Palgrave Studies in Global Citizenship Education and Democracy

Series Editor

Jason Laker
San Jose State University
San Jose, California, USA

Aim of the Series

This series will engage with the theoretical and practical debates regarding citizenship, human rights education, social inclusion, and individual and group identities as they relate to the role of higher and adult education on an international scale. Books in the series will consider hopeful possibilities for the capacity of higher and adult education to enable citizenship, human rights, democracy and the common good, including emerging research and interesting and effective practices. It will also participate in and stimulate deliberation and debate about the constraints, barriers and sources and forms of resistance to realizing the promise of egalitarian Civil Societies. The series will facilitate continued conversation on policy and politics, curriculum and pedagogy, review and reform, and provide a comparative overview of the different conceptions and approaches to citizenship education and democracy around the world.

More information about this series at
http://www.springer.com/series/14625

Catherine Broom
Editor

Youth Civic Engagement in a Globalized World

Citizenship Education in Comparative Perspective

palgrave
macmillan

Editor
Catherine Broom
University of British Columbia-Okanagan
Canada

Palgrave Studies in Global Citizenship Education and Democracy
ISBN 978-1-137-56532-7   ISBN 978-1-137-56533-4   (eBook)
DOI 10.1057/978-1-137-56533-4

Library of Congress Control Number: 2016947001

Cover illustration: © Horizon International Images Limited / Alamy Stock Photo

Printed on acid-free paper

This Palgrave Macmillan imprint is published by Springer Nature
The registered company is Nature America Inc.
The registered company address is: 1 New York Plaza, New York, NY 10004, U.S.A.

*To my mom, dad, and sisters, who taught me about what to value
in life, to Sal, who shares life's joys and challenges with me, and to
David, who inspires my drive for a better world for his future.
To all those who work towards developing a more caring
and compassionate world rooted in respect for others
and the world.*

Acknowledgements

Thank you to all of the chapter authors who worked hard to submit their chapters on time. I would also like to acknowledge the Faculty of Education at University of British Columbia (UBC) Okanagan for their support and Parul Kathuria for her research assistance help.

CONTENTS

ABOUT THE AUTHORS

Catherine Broom is an assistant professor in the Faculty of Education at UBC Okanagan, Canada. Her work focuses on the areas of local and global citizenship, history of education, and social studies education. She is the journal editor of *Citizenship Education Research Journal* (CERJ).

Enzo Colombo is Professor of Sociology of culture at the University of Milan, Italy. His most recent book is *Children of Immigrant in a Globalized World. A Generational Experience* (with. P. Rebughini) (2012).

Douglas Fleming is an associate professor with the Faculty of Education at the University of Ottawa, Canada. His work focuses on critical and post-structural aspects of English as a Second Language (ESL), language assessment, citizenship, equity, qualitative research, and policy development.

Richard Harris is Associate Professor of History Education at the University of Reading, UK. He taught in secondary schools for many years and has been involved in teacher education for 15 years. He has researched and written a number of articles and chapters about issues relating to history education and citizenship.

Liz Jackson is Assistant Professor in Education at the University of Hong Kong. Her research areas include civic and moral education, multicultural education, and global studies in education.

Puja Kapai is Associate Professor of Law and Director of the Centre for Comparative and Public Law at the University of Hong Kong. She publishes on minority rights and citizenship theory.

Ching Yin Leung is a research officer in the Education Policy Unit (EPU) at University of Hong Kong. Her research interests include education policy, IT & education, and extensive reading.

Anthony Di Mascio is an associate professor in the School of Education at Bishop's University, Canada. His research interests are in the history and politics of education in Canada.

Tania Naanous graduated from International Relations at Universidad Iberoamericana. Her internships include the Mexican Council of Foreign Relations and the Organization of American States (OAS). Currently, she collaborates with the Mexico Research Center for Peace (CIPMEX) and she is a Consultant at Radar Digital. Her topics of interest include gender equality, democracy, and political communication.

Keiichi Takaya is an associate professor in the Faculty of Letters, Kokugakuin University, Japan. His research interests are in the philosophical and historical foundations of education, such as the influence of Pestalozzianism in the development of teacher education programs in North America.

Medardo Tapia Uribe is a researcher at CRIM, UNAM in Mexico, and a former research associate and Harvard University doctoral graduate Fulbright Scholar (1989). He is currently doing research in Río De Janeiro, Medellín, and Cuidad Juárez as resilient communities before violence.

Vanessa Tse completed her graduate work at the University of Victoria, and her research interests include holistic education, resilience, spirituality, and poetic inquiry. She currently lives in India where she works in two children's homes that care for orphaned and destitute children.

Shiru Wang currently teaches at the University of Hong Kong. Her research focuses on political attitudes and behaviour in China, particularly online activism, corruption tolerance, and voting behaviour.

LIST OF FIGURES

LIST OF TABLES

CHAPTER 1

Youth Civic Engagement in Context

Catherine Broom

Citizenship education is a thriving field of study in many democratic nations. Indeed, scholars, policy makers, and practitioners often justify the field's importance by arguing that participatory citizenship is the foundation of democratic societies (Dewey, 1916).

Recently, much citizenship education literature has disparaged youth participation in civic life, arguing that youth are both apathetic and disengaged (such as Arthur & Davies, 2008; Beaumont, 2010; Campbell-Patton & Quinn Patton, 2010; Finlay, Wray-Lake, & Flanagan, 2010; Gidengil, Blais, Nevitte, & Nadeau, 2004; Howe, 2010; Levine & Higins-D'Alessandro, 2010; Putnam, 1995). For example, Howe (2010), in *Citizens Adrift: The Democratic Disengagement of Young Canadians*, argues that Canadian youth are less politically engaged due to declining interest and less community-mindedness.

In this book, the authors explore this apparent decline in youth civic engagement through research studies conducted in seven societies/ nations with varied experiences with democracy. This work is framed within a youth civic engagement model, which is described in this chapter.

C. Broom (✉)
Faculty of Education, University of British Columbia Okanagan,
Kelowna, BC, Canada
e-mail: catherine.broom@ubc.ca

© The Author(s) 2017
C. Broom (ed.), *Youth Civic Engagement in a Globalized World*,
Palgrave Studies in Global Citizenship Education and Democracy,
DOI 10.1057/978-1-137-56533-4_1

1

The findings for each nation/society are presented in separate chapters, along with contextual and historical discussions of citizenship education. Chapter 2 describes Canada's citizenship education history and context and the findings of the study conducted there. The findings for England are presented in Chap. 3, followed by those of Hong Kong in Chap. 4. India is discussed in Chap. 5, and Italy in Chap. 6. Japan's findings are described in Chap. 7 and Mexico in Chap. 8. The last chapter of the book summarizes and discusses major findings.

Currently, with due acknowledgement of supra-national and global forces such as the flow of capital and of alternative conceptualizations of citizenship such as global or cosmopolitan citizenship (Apiah, 2007; Nussbaum, 1997), nation states are the major means through which space is divided, and within which social–cultural, economic, political, and ideological structures are often negotiated and contained. Thus, this book explores how citizenship is understood within six nation states that have varied connections to democracy. The book also explores one society, Hong Kong, which had democratic connections and is now part of China. The chapter on Hong Kong illustrates how citizenship does not necessarily equate to nationhood. Multiple and contested conceptions of citizenship may be contained within nation states, and certain conceptions of citizenship may spread beyond political borders.

KEY TERMS

Citizenship can be conceived in varying ways, depending on ideology and culture (Arnot, Araújo, Deliyanni-Kouimtzis, Ivinson, & Tomé, 2000). For example, teachers in varied nations have different conceptions of the "citizen" they are trying to educate, including the dutiful, critical, skeptical, caring, good, and protesting citizen (Arnot et al., 2000). Bennett, Freelon, and Wells (2010) describe "dutiful citizens" as those who participate in traditional governance structures and are taught in a top down manner. This is compared to "actualizing citizens" who actively create their own meanings through and with social media.

Westheimer and Kahne (2004), drawing from their research of American citizenship education programs, describe three kinds of citizens: the personally responsible citizen supports his or her community through behaviors that are service oriented (such as donating money), the participatory citizen is actively involved in civic life, and the justice-oriented citizen aims to increase social justice in society.

Heater's (2004) conceptual model of a cube of citizenship illustrates varied features associated with the concept. Along one side, he identifies the elements of citizenship (identity, virtue, legal/civil, political, and social). These are connected to geographical levels along a second side, ranging from provincial to global scales. The third side of the cube encompasses educational elements: the necessary knowledge, attitudes, and skills citizens require.

We take a broad conception of citizenship drawing from Marshall's (1950) civic, political, and social conceptions of citizenship. Civic citizenship relates to the legal freedoms and rights citizens enjoy, political citizenship to participation in political processes, and social citizenship to institutional and other support provided to individuals. Citizenship is argued to be a feeling of association with and connection to, and within, a particular social group, which includes civic, social, and political elements, processes, and/or institutions. Although citizenship is often equated to being a citizen of a nation, our definition of citizenship as a sense of connection within a particular social group that leads to particular attitudes and actions does not necessarily equate to national boundaries or spatial borders. The multi-tiered nature of citizenship is illustrated in societies featuring multiple levels of political belonging, from local level communities to national and global communities. For instance, in Hong Kong, national (Mainland China) and regional (Hong Kong level) perspectives and commitments in political and cultural belonging can be seen to compete with one another.

Active citizenship refers to youth's social, political, or civic actions in their societies or nations, and civic engagement refers to interest and participation in civic, political, or social activities, such as voting, volunteering, or joining a civic group. When youth engage in civic, political, and social processes through multiple means, they are empowered.

CURRENT RESEARCH AND OUR CONCEPTUAL MODEL

Educational research has explored (1) the multiple meanings of citizenship, citizenship practices, and citizenship education (such as Arthur and Davies, 2008; Levinson, 2010: Sherrod et al., 2002; Sherrod, Torney-Purta, & Flanagan, 2010); (2) the relations between citizenship education and tensions at the level of the nation (Banks, 2007; Callan, 1997; Sears, 2009; Zajda, Holger, & Saha, 2009); and (3) the influences of globalization on citizenship (Apiah, 2007; Nussbaum, 1997; Reid, Gill, & Sears, 2010).

Limited work in education, however, has theorized the features and processes of youth civic engagement, that is, how youth's internal and external factors may influence their civic attitudes and behaviors. Levine (2007) describes one of the few studies in this area that asked students to choose a personality type that best described them. The research concluded that how individuals labeled themselves affected their future actions.

Other scholars have explored youth's sense of self-efficacy, relating this to government knowledge, youth's sense of agency and self-efficacy, and their connections to others (Bandura, 1997; Beaumont, 2010; Fox, Mediratta, Ruglis, Stoudt, Shah, & Shah, 2010; Rubin, 2007; Russell, Toomey, Crockett, & Laub, 2010; Torney-Purta, Amadeo, & Andolina, 2010 Youniss & Levine, 2009).

Education scholars, however, have not yet developed a complete model of how internal and external factors may influence youth actions. In *Roots of Civic Identity*, Yates and Youniss (2006) begin the process by describing how the field has moved from a political socialization perspective to a more nuanced understanding of how individuals construct their civic and social understanding through their interactions in society. The field has moved away from a socialization, direct internalization perspective to one that acknowledges the active manner in which individuals construct their understanding. However, these authors do not go far enough in recognizing the implications of individuals constructing their civic beliefs. The logical extension to this theory is to understand how individuals vary in the personal traits and character and how these may further influence and affect developing civic attitudes and behaviors. For example, the authors discuss research that finds that youth who are more active in their high school years are more active adults. These authors do not consider what internal factors might be responsible for these more active behaviors. In other words, it is possible that these youth are more active as they have leadership traits and values that emphasize social interaction.

In short, previous work conceptualizing youth civic actions in the field of education is limited, and it is not contained in a comprehensive model that considers both internal and external factors and their interaction and how these influence youth attitudes and actions. Research that pays attention to these factors is growing in other fields.

Studies in Political Science, Psychology, and Management

Earlier in the twentieth century, Political Science studies used to focus on exploring socialization in relation to the development of political participation. Recently, however, more researchers are beginning to give greater attention to individuals' unique characteristics (Dinsen, Norgaard, & Klemmensen, 2014). In their study, Dinsen et al. (2014) explored the relations between personality traits using the Big Five Model and civic behaviors. They found that people who were more agreeable and open tended to have higher levels of social trust. In contrast, people who were more neurotic or conscientious tended to have lower levels of social trust. They also found that more conscientious people tended to engage in more traditional civic activities, and more agreeable people tried to understand how other people think more.

Researchers in areas such as Psychology, Social Work, and Business have also conducted studies related to individuals' characters and civic life. Omoto, Snyder, and Hacket (2010) found that individuals who engage in community service tended to have a communal orientation and were extroverted. Borman, Penner, Allen, Motowidlo, and Stephan (2001) concluded that personality traits such as conscientiousness, agreeableness, and dependability were more highly correlated to citizenship performance in relation to individuals' jobs and that locus of control, communitarianism, and personal initiative also influenced behavior. Christens (2012) added a relational component to Zimmerman's (1995) psychological empowerment model which included emotional, cognitive, and behavioral elements. We build on this work through the development of a youth civic engagement model that considers both internal and external factors and their interactions.

THEORETICAL WORK UPON WHICH WE BUILD

Bronfenbrenner's (1979, 2005) ecological systems theory suggests that individuals interact with a number of systems, which also interact with each other (Wilkenfeld, Lauckhardt, & Torney-Purta, 2010). These include the microsystem, mesosystem, exosystem, and macrosystem. The microsystem encompasses those environmental elements that directly influence a person, such as their family, schools, and friends. The mesosystem encompasses the interactions between the individual and the microsystem, the context around the person, and the interactions between various systems and how these then influence the individual. More indirect influences, such as local policies, exist in the exosystem. Finally, general social and cultural influences, such as globalization, are found in the macrosystem.

Positive Youth Development Theory

Drawing from ecological systems theory, positive youth development theory argues that development, understood as individual transformational change, is a function of the interaction of youth's internal and external variables (Overton, 2010). The system is "open, active, transforming, self-organizing, and self-regulating" (Overton, 2010, p. 1970) and is represented as context ←→ individual, meaning that external factors and conditions influence internal factors, and internal factors and conditions influence external factors; they are "mutually constitutive" (Overton, 2010, p. 1992). Biological, social, and individual factors interact, co-act, co-influence, "co-construct," and "co-evolve" (p. 1992). External conditions and factors include the various systems described by Bronfrenbrener, from local contexts (family, school friends) to larger social, cultural, and even historical factors. As the theory is embedded in a process-based understanding of change and includes history (i.e. a time variable), individuals can change, that is, they are in the process of "becoming" (Overton, 2010, p. 1980). Further, individuals can develop through multiple means, as developmental change is emergent and context- and individual-based. Individuals' actions provide feedback to the youth that influence further development and actions in a cyclical manner, leading to a continual transformational process. In a civic sense, the theory aims to develop youth's civic attitudes and involvement through the provision of contextual factors that positively influence youth development (Cargo, Grams, Ottoson, Ward, & Green, 2003; Sherrod, 2007).

Youth Civic Behaviors and Attitudes: Interactions and Complexity

Building from ecological systems theory and positive youth development theory, our conceptual model of youth civic behavior considers a number of variables together and their interaction. The model theorizes that people are born with varying traits and that they develop in various ways depending on the interactions between their internal and external factors. Thus, youth's attitudes and actions in civic life may differ, based on the manner in which individuals' personality traits, attitudes, and beliefs interact with their experiences and their sociocultural environments. Individuals' sense of duty or care for others and their optimism or pessimism, for example, may influence how they perceive and, thus, how they act, in civic life. Factors internal to a person interact with external experiences to determine civic action (Model 1).

Our Conceptual Model

Within the person, we consider: personality types and traits, such as being analytical, caring, and/or optimistic. This includes an individual's unique character traits, which are fairly fixed, and his/her more modifiable, ascribed labels. These labels have come to be applied to (or accepted by) the individual as a result of his/her experiences. Other internal factors include gender, identity (Crocetti, Jahromi, & Meeus, 2012), and attitudes and values that can include patriotism, views of community (individual-focused or community-minded focused [Omoto et al., 2010]), and empathy (Russell et al., 2010). Further factors include motives or aims, which can be influenced by, or stem from, family, friends, religion, cultural/communal factors, or conceptions of duty among others; confidence and sense of efficacy, or belief in one's own abilities; and knowledge and skills (such as communicative skills [Lee, Shah, & McLeod, 2013]). Knowledge and skills include individuals' structuring discourses or ideologies (Mayo, 2004) and cultures.

External influences include direct experiences on a person, such as family (Lenzi, 2014), friends, and school experiences. Experiences also come from the community, local laws, or local associations and social–economic context including the wealth of, and issues in, the local community. Other influences include the environment, culture, society (including the dominant ideologies or discourses [Mayo, 2004]), as well as international influences or experiences, such as pop culture, the media, and globalization. These influences act simultaneously and in complex ways on the individual and with each other. A factor that is closer to an individual does not make it necessarily stronger. A factor such as culture or global trends (in technology [social media] or pop culture, for instance) can be as significant as a factor close to a person (Fig. 1.1).

In this model, youth develop a certain civic mindset, which is the product of the interaction of their internal and external factors. When an event occurs in the youth's environment, the individual processes the event through his/her current civic mindset, and he/she acts on the basis of this cognition. The person then receives feedback from this action that helps to determine how he/she acts in the future.

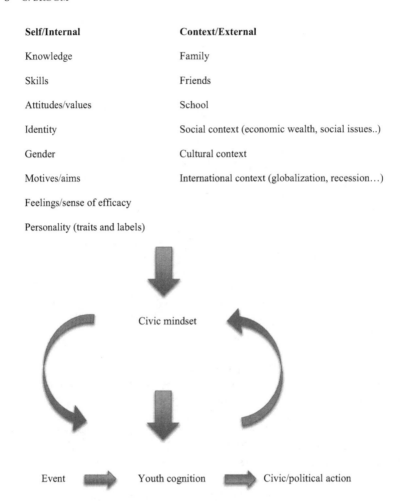

Self/Internal	Context/External
Knowledge	Family
Skills	Friends
Attitudes/values	School
Identity	Social context (economic wealth, social issues..)
Gender	Cultural context
Motives/aims	International context (globalization, recession…)
Feelings/sense of efficacy	
Personality (traits and labels)	

Civic mindset

Event → Youth cognition → Civic/political action

Fig. 1.1   Model of youth civic engagement

Sherrod (2007) argues that six Cs are significant factors in civic behaviors: competence, confidence, character, connection, caring, and contribution. In our model, competence relates to knowledge and skills, confidence to a sense of efficacy, and character to attitudes/values and personality/traits. Connection relates to youth's feelings toward the various social spaces they are found within (family, school, society/culture…), and their identities and bonds to these spaces (i.e. how do they identify themselves in relation to these various social spaces and how much they feel a part of them). Finally, caring relates to youth's feelings and attitudes to these social spaces and connects to aims.

LENS AND IMPLICATIONS OF OUR MODEL

As the model conceptualizes action to emerge from the interaction of internal and external factors with experiences undertaken and then processed, youth's civic mindsets can change when their life experiences or social contexts change. Youth, in other words, actively construct their citizenship through their lived experiences. This helps to explain why research in the USA has shown that youth disengagement can become young adult engagement once young adults settle into adult lives, with work and homes (Flanagan & Levine, 2010). Youth can also belong to varying sub-cultures, which can also influence their conceptions of and participation in civic life. Engagement exists when the combination of experience and internal processing leads to civic action.

Education may influence individuals in several ways. Firstly, it can provide experiences, with reflection, that allow individuals to re-think their views, and thus change their beliefs. Secondly, it can provide knowledge, skills, and exposure to different attitudes that can also change a person. Thirdly, education can influence individuals' self-ascribed labels and sense of self-efficacy—and thus change individuals' civic attitudes and behaviors.

This conceptual model was used as the basis of a research study with youth conducted in seven nations/societies. These nations were randomly chosen as they have varied experiences with democracy and different social, economic, and cultural contexts. The aim was to develop insights into how varied contexts may influence youth's developing civic attitudes and behaviors and the role that internal and external factors in varied social and cultural spaces may play in the development of youth's civic attitudes and behaviors.

RESEARCH STUDY

The authors developed survey and interview research tools to explore youth's conceptions of, and participation in, civic life and the relations between these and the conceptual model just described. The anonymous surveys collected relevant demographic information (age/race/gender/class/citizenship) and asked participants to select their free time and civic activities. Participants were asked to comment on their knowledge and views of government/politics, democracy and public participation, their ideal political state, and how they envisioned general public and their own participation in civic life. Youth were also asked to select which personality they believed they were and to identify which traits they associated themselves with. Personality types were divided into traits that included leader/motivated, friendly/positive, people-focused (caring)/outgoing, and introverted/organized.[1]

The study's main questions were:

What are the characteristics of youth civic engagement/disengagement in nations/societies with different experiences with democracy?

How does engagement relate to individuals' internal and external factors, such as knowledge, attitudes, characteristics, experiences, and cultures?

What recommendations emerge from the findings?

The research tools were piloted and then refined based on feedback. Scholars provided recommendations on how to amend the survey tool prior to using it in their nations, in order to address any social or cultural factors. Data analysis was carried out using SPSS software. The researchers ran descriptive statistics and explored correlations between factors using cross-tabs. Open-ended questions were coded and grouped into themes using a grounded theory approach (Glaser, 1992).

RESEARCH CHALLENGES AND LIMITATIONS

In all nations, the researchers ran into data collection challenges. In Canada, recruiting youth participants in some data collection sites that aimed to collect varied youth perspectives was difficult. For example, ads were placed in national online magazines, but the response rate to these was low. Getting youth to agree to be interviewed in the UK, Italy, Japan, and Canada was also difficult, even when incentives such as honorariums were given, so the data analysis presented in this book is focused on the survey findings.

In each nation, the number of youth who participated were limited (about 150 youth participated in most nations), and data were collected in few locations. The researchers do not make the claim that they are presenting the overall "voice" of youth in their nation/society. Rather, they are presenting a small "glimmer" of information about some youth. Further, as these youth were those who consented to participate in the study, they are most likely not a representative sample. They maybe youth who are more likely to hold strong views toward civic life, and—according to previous work (Howe, 2010)—are also more likely to be youth who are educated. Indeed, most of the data were collected from university youth. Youth in other sub-groups may hold very different perspectives to those described in this book. Future research can explore whether youth in varied sub-groups hold different civic attitudes and participate in different activities.

The researchers acknowledge the complexity of citizenship, citizenship education, and youth beliefs and attitudes. They aim to provide some insights based on the data they have collected, and to reflect on the model presented in this chapter in order to begin an initial analysis of the connections between lived experiences and youth civic attitudes and behaviors.

NOTE

1. Modified from: http://workawesome.com/communication/4-personality-types/#more-18836

REFERENCES

Apiah, K. (2007). *Cosmopolitanism: Ethics in a world of strangers.* New York: Norton and Co.

Arnot, M., Araújo, H., Deliyanni-Kouimtzis, K., Ivinson, G., & Tomé, A. (2000). The good citizen: Cultural understandings of citizenship and gender amongst a new generation of teachers. In M. Leicester, C. Modgil, & S. Modgil (Eds.), *Politics, education and citizenship* (pp. 217–231). London: Falmer press.

Arthur, J., & Davies, I. (Eds.) (2008). *Citizenship education.* London: Sage.

Bandura, A. (1997). *Self-efficacy: The exercise of control.* New York: Freeman.

Banks, J. (2007). *Diversity and citizenship education: Global perspectives.* San Francisco, CA: Jossey Bass.

Beaumont, E. (2010). Political agency and empowerment: Pathways for developing a sense of political efficacy in young adults. In L. Sherrod, J. Torney-Purta, & C. Flanagan (Eds.), *Handbook of research on civic engagement* (pp. 525–558). Hoboken, NJ: John Wiley & Sons.

Bennett, W., Freelon, D., & Wells, C. (2010). Changing citizen identity and the rise of a participatory media culture. In L. Sherrod, J. Torney-Purta, & C. Flanagan (Eds.), *Handbook of research on civic engagement* (pp. 393–423). Hoboken, NJ: John Wiley & Sons.

Borman, W., Penner, L., Allen, T., & Motowidlo, S. (2001). Personality predictors of citizenship performance. *International Journal of Selection and Assessment, 9*(1), 52–69.

Bronfenbrenner, U. (1979). *The ecology of human development.* Cambridge, MA: Harvard University Press.

Bronfenbrenner, U. (2005). *Making human beings human: Bioecological perspectives on human development.* Thousand Oaks, CA: Sage Publications.

Callan, E. (1997). *Creating citizens: Political education and liberal democracy.* Oxford: Clarendon Press.

Campbell-Patton, C., & Quinn Patton, M. (2010). Conceptualizing and evaluating the complexities of youth civic engagement. In L. Sherrod, J. Torney-Purta, & C. Flanagan (Eds.), *Handbook of research on civic engagement* (pp. 593–619). Hoboken, NJ: John Wiley & Sons.

Cargo, M., Grams, G., Ottoson, J., Ward, P., & Green, L. (2003). Empowerment as fostering positive youth development and citizenship. *American Journal of Health Behavior, 27,* S66–S79.

Christens, B. (2012). Towards relational empowerment. *American Journal Community Psychology, 50,* 114–128.

Crocetti, E., Jahromi, P., & Meeus, W. (2012). Identity and civic engagement in adolescence. *Journal of Adolescence, 35,* 521–532.

Dewey, J. (1916). *Democracy and education.* New York: Macmillan Co.

Dinesen, P., Norgaard, A., & Klemmensen, R. (2014). The civic personality: Personality and democratic citizenship. *Political Studies, 62*(S1), 134–152.

Finlay, A., Wray-Lake, L., & Flanagan, C. (2010). Civic engagement during the transition to adulthood: Developmental opportunities and social policies at a critical juncture. In L. Sherrod, J. Torney-Purta, & C. Flanagan (Eds.), *Handbook of research on civic engagement* (pp. 393–423). Hoboken, NJ: John Wiley & Sons.

Flanagan, C., & Levine, P. (2010). Civic engagement and the transition to adulthood. In *The Future of Children* .Retrieved from https://www.princeton.edu/futureofchildren/publications/docs/20_01_08.pdf

Fox, M., Mediratta, K., Ruglis, J., Stoudt, B., Shah, S., & Fine, M. (2010). Critical youth engagement: Participatory action research and organizing. In L. Sherrod, J. Torney-Purta, & C. Flanagan (Eds.), *Handbook of research on civic engagement* (pp. 621–649). Hoboken, NJ: John Wiley & Sons.

Gidengil, E., Blais, A., Nevitte, N., & Nadeau, R. (2004). *Citizens.* Vancouver: UBC Press.

Glaser, B. (1992). *Basics of grounded theory analysis.* Mill Valley, CA: Sociology Press.

Heater, D. (2004). *Citizenship: The civic ideal in world history, politics andeducation* (3rd ed.). Manchester: Manchester University Press.

Howe, P. (2010). *Citizens adrift: The democratic disengagement of young Canadians.* Vancouver: UBC Press.

Lee, N., Shah, D., & McLeod, J. (2013). Processes of political socialization: A communication mediation approach to youth civic engagement. *Communication Research, 40*(5), 669–697.

Lenzi, M. (2014). The role played by the family in shaping early and middle adolescent civic responsibility. *The Journal of Early Adolescence, 34*(2), 251.

Levine, P. (2007). *The future of democracy: Developing the next generation of American citizens.* Medford, MA: Tufts University Press.

Levine, P., & Higins-D'Alessandro, A. (2010). Youth civic engagement: Normative issues. In L. Sherrod, J. Torney-Purta, & C. Flanagan (Eds.), *Handbook of research on civic engagement* (pp. 221–248). Hoboken, NJ: John Wiley & Sons.

Levinson, M. (2010). The civic empowerment gap: Defining the problem and locating solutions. In L. Sherrod, J. Torney-Purta, & C. Flanagan (Eds.), *Handbook of research on civic engagement* (pp. 115–137). Hoboken, NJ: John Wiley & Sons.

Marshall, T. H. (1950). *Citizenship and social class and other essays.* Cambridge: Cambridge University Press.

Mayo, M. (2004). Exclusion, inclusion, and empowerment: Community empowerment? Reflecting on the lessons of strategies to promote empowerment. In J. Anderson & B. Siim (Eds.), *Politics of inclusion and empowerment: Gender, class, and citizenship* (pp. 139–158). London: Palgrave Macmillan.

Nussbaum, M. (1997). *Cultivating humanity: A classical defense of reform in liberal education.* Cambridge, MA: Harvard University Press.

Omoto, A., Snyder, M., & Hackett, J. (2010). Personality and motivational antecedents of activism and civic engagement. *Journal of Personality, 78*(6), 1703–1734.

Overton, W. F. (2010). Life-span development: Concepts and issues. In R. M. Lerner (Ed-in-chief) & W. F. Overton (Vol. Ed.), *The handbook of life-span development: Vol. 1. Cognition, biology, and methods* (pp. 1–29). Hoboken, NJ: Wiley.

Putnam, R. (1995). Bowling along: America's declining social capital. *Journal of Democracy, 6*(1), 65–78 Retrieved from http://xroads.virginia.edu/~HYPER/detoc/assoc/bowling.html.

Reid, A., Gill, J., & Sears, A. (2010). *Globalization, the nation-state and the citizen: Dilemmas and directions for civics and citizenship education.* New York: Routledge.

Rubin, B. (2007). 'There's still not justice': Youth civic identity development amid distinct school and community contexts. *Teachers College Record, 109*, 449–481.

Russell, S. T., Toomey, R., Crockett, J., & Laub, C. (2010). LGBT politics, youth activism and civic engagement. In L. Sherrod, J. Torney-Purta, & C. Flanagan (Eds.), *Handbook of research on civic engagement* (pp. 471–494). Hoboken, NJ: John Wiley & Sons.

Sears, A. (2009). Special issue: Canadian perspectives on democracy, diversity and citizenship education. *Citizenship Teaching and Learning, 5*(2), 1–107. http://www.citized.info/pdf/eJournal/5%202%20final.pdf

Sherrod, L. (2007). Civic engagement as an expression of positive youth development. In R. Silbereisen & R. Lerner (Eds.), *Approaches to positive youth development* (pp. 59–74). London: Sage.

Sherrod, L., Flanagan, C., & Youniss, J. (2002). Growing into citizenship: Multiple pathways and diverse influences. *Applied Developmental Science, 6*(4), 172–173.

Sherrod, L., Torney-Purta, J., & Flanagan, C. (Eds.) (2010). *Handbook of research on civic engagement*. Hoboken, NJ: John Wiley & Sons.

Torney-Purta, J., Amadeo, J., & Andolina, M. (2010). A conceptual framework and multimethod approach for research on political socialization and civic engagement. In L. Sherrod, J. Torney-Purta, & C. Flanagan (Eds.), *Handbook of research on civic engagement* (pp. 393–423). Hoboken, NJ: John Wiley & Sons.

Westheimer, J., & Kahne, J. (2004). What kind of citizen? The politics of educating for democracy. *American Educational Research Journal, 41*(2), 237–269.

Wilkenfeld, B., Lauckhardt, J., & Torney-Purta, J. (2010). The relation between developmental theory and measures of civic engagement in research on adolescents. In L. Sherrod, J. Torney-Purta, & C. Flanagan (Eds.), *Handbook of research on civic engagement* (pp. 193–219). Hoboken, NJ: John Wiley & Sons.

Yates, M., & Youniss, J. (2006). *Roots of civic identity: International perspectives on community service and activism in youth*. Cambridge: Cambridge University Press.

Youniss, J., & Levine, P. (2009). *Engaging young people in civic life*. Nashville, TN: Vanderbilt University Press.

Zajda, J., Holger, D., & Saha, L. (Eds.) (2009). *Nation-building, identity and citizenship education: Cross cultural perspectives series*. Dordrecht: Springer.

CHAPTER 2

Citizenship Education in Canada, Past and Present

Catherine Broom, Anthony Di Mascio,
and Douglas Fleming

After reviewing the history of citizenship education in Canada, this chapter describes the findings of the Canadian study of youth's conceptions of, and actions toward, citizenship.

CURRENT CONTEXT

Canadian youth are growing up in uncertain times and they are aware of this. A nation-wide study found that youth's major concerns were lack of employment prospects, costs of education and student debt, costs of living, and the environment (MacLean, 2012; Morrison, 2013). Young

C. Broom (✉)
Faculty of Education, University of British Columbia Okanagan,
Kelowna, BC, Canada
e-mail: catherine.broom@ubc.ca

A. Di Mascio
School of Education, Bishop's University, Sherbrooke, QC, Canada

D. Fleming
Faculty of Education, University of Ottawa, Ottawa, ON, Canada

© The Author(s) 2017
C. Broom (ed.), *Youth Civic Engagement in a Globalized World*,
Palgrave Studies in Global Citizenship Education and Democracy,
DOI 10.1057/978-1-137-56533-4_2

Canadians are also challenging conventional social norms. For example, according to these studies, most youth support the legalization of marijuana, and 50% are using or have used the drug.

The survey data were collected during a time of global economic insecurity and concerns over terrorism. Canada maintained a level of social and economic stability under the ten-year governance of Conservative Prime Minister Harper; however, signs emerged that the public was ready for a change. The media increasingly disparaged Harper's government over Senate spending scandals. A new election race was called at the end of the Summer in 2015.

The federal election was held in October 2015. It led to the dramatic defeat of the Conservatives and the election of the young, Liberal Justin Trudeau. Trudeau won due to his support from immigrants and youth, with his promises to reform Conservative changes to bills that were viewed by ethnic minorities as taking away their rights, bring some Syrian refugees to Canada, spend more on infrastructure, and legalize marijuana (Levinson King, 2015). The study data were collected before, during, and after this Federal election and demonstrate how youth—at least the youth surveyed here—engaged with the electoral process and demonstrated their desire for change.

THE HISTORY OF CITIZENSHIP EDUCATION IN CANADA

Developing citizens has been one of the main goals of public schools (Cordasco, 1976). Citizenship education has generally been political education, and the good citizen has been understood to be a passive supporter of the current government, who has good work values (Osborne, 1996). In some provinces and times, citizenship education has been integrated into history or social studies classes. In others, it has been taught separately.

As education is a provincial matter in Canada, each province designs and implements its own curricula. At the same time, however, there are similar trends across the nation (Broom, 2008). Our historical review illustrates connections between curriculum reform and changing social, political, and economic conditions.

NATIONAL TRENDS IN CITIZENSHIP EDUCATION

In 1867, four British colonies joined together to make "Canada." The nation's laws were framed within the British North American Act, establishing an English colonial nation, with some rights for its French population.

The native population was largely ignored in the process, pushed onto reserves and discriminatorily "managed" through the Indian Act.

After Confederation, schools were identified as places where nationalism could be fostered. Thus, early textbooks aimed to build patriotism through positive, "nation-building" narratives (Francis, 1997; Wertsch, 2002). Schools also aimed to assimilate diverse groups to British traditions (Broom, 2011; Osborne, 1996).

During the early twentieth century, immigration was encouraged (Troper, 2002). Varied ethnic groups in schools attempted to both integrate and resist assimilationist values, building their own complex identities (Bruno Joffre, 1998). Workers actively campaigned for improved working conditions. Aboriginal children were forced into residential schools, with devastating consequences for these children, their families, and communities.

Canadians followed American trends in establishing the subject of social studies in the 1930s. The subject variously aimed to teach citizenship through history or integrated social sciences study (Broom & Evans, 2015; Jorgensen, 2012). Social studies emphasized social citizenship, that is, character or values education in conjunction with being "good" community citizens who voted and participated in the community.

After World War II, population and the economy grew. Groups pushed for increased human rights protection as a result of the Holocaust and the signing of the UN Declaration of Human Rights (Patrias, 2006; Troper, 2002). Canada became an independent nation from the UK. Human rights movements in the 1960s and French Canadians' active fight for increased national self-determination led to increased Federal recognition of French Canadians rights and paved the way for the establishment of multiculturalism and the Canadian Charter of Rights and Freedoms (Troper, 2002; Osborne, 1996).

In the 1970s, increased attention was given to Canadian Studies (Clarke, 2004; Tomkins, 1986), and in the 1980s, curricula aimed to develop students' acceptance of inclusion and multiculturalism and their support of global citizenship and the environment (Broom, 2008; Osborne, 1996).

Citizenship education has pushed students to be "active" citizens in the "progressive/meliorist" or Deweyian (1938) sense (Broom & Evans, 2015; Sears & Hughes, 1996). More social justice and transformative notions of citizenship education (Evans, 2004) are found, in limited form, in more recent citizenship education curricula (Broom, 2013;

Broom & Evans, 2015). These aim to have students understand the injustices various groups have suffered in Canada's past and present and to actively work to address these injustices. For example, some curricula recognize the injustices suffered by Aboriginal peoples as a result of colonial and post-colonial policies and racism.

HISTORY OF CITIZENSHIP EDUCATION IN BRITISH COLUMBIA

Prior to 1930, citizenship education was integrated into history. Citizenship education taught students an assimilationist, "nation building" story of Canada that aimed to develop patriotism and knowledge of government structures and processes in order to develop "good citizens" who voted (Broom, 2008; Russell, 2002).

British Columbia's (BC) 1919 curriculum, for example, integrated civics into history instruction. The text *Canadian Civics* (Jenkins, 1918) portrayed the government in a positive light. It described the structures and processes of government and citizens' responsibilities such as being "active" by voting, joining a political party, preventing corruptive practices in the government, and "assist[ing] ....all good causes" (Jenkins, 1918, p. 169).

In the 1930s, social studies was implemented. Citizenship education was integrated into social studies (Osborne, 1996; Broom, 2011). In the 1950s, reaction to progressivism, advocacy of traditional values, and the Cold War and Sputnik led to fears that students were not being prepared well enough to compete with the Soviet Union and resulted in the release of a new curriculum guide in 1968. It focused equally on history and geography education using Bruner' structure of disciplines theory. Citizenship education was given less direct attention, with the focus being inquiry-based learning.

Social (increasing cultural diversity) and economic change (economic restraint) led to the 1985 curriculum revision. One of its aims was educating good citizens. The guides included the same content on political (governmental) and legal structures and processes, with more attention to multiculturalism, human rights and global geography and interdependence, and skills development framed largely within a social history course (Russell, 2002; Troper, 2002; Osborne, 1996).

At the end of the twentieth century, curricula were revised again (Ministry of Education, British Columbia, 1997). The civic goal of social studies was reiterated, although little citizenship content was included in the curriculum, which remained largely history. A unit on the government of Canada in grade 11 had students study Canada's political and legal structures, citizen's responsibilities, and social issues.

In 2005, BC implemented a new Civics 11 course (Ministry of Education, British Columbia, 2005), with similar topics to the 1919 civics textbook: learning about government structures and the responsibilities of citizens and learning how to get "actively" involved by voting or participating in an issue of interest. Changes had to do with taking a more critical look at Canada's past and present and focusing more on skill development (Broom & Evans, 2015).

Currently, academic discussion around citizenship education focuses on pluralism, multiculturalism, identity, and how to balance tensions between diversity and social cohesion and nationalism and globalism (Herbert, 2002). There is also a resurgence of interest in history education (Seixas, 2004).

CITIZENSHIP EDUCATION IN ONTARIO

Previous periods of citizenship education in Ontario focused on the conception of a fixed and stratified political hierarchy in which the "political subjects were not seen as self-creating" (Curtis, 1988, p. 102). Citizenship was taught deductively as sets of received unproblematic precepts pertaining to deference to authority.

In the 1960s, this orientation began to break down into a growing recognition that citizenship is a complex, multidimensional concept. A more interdisciplinary approach became predominant in which every secondary course was meant to treat citizenship in order to produce a new and distinct definition of what it meant to be Canadian in the face of modern multicultural realities. This change is reflected in the Ontario Ministry of Education Social Sciences Study Committee, 1962 recommendation that teachers prepare students to discuss citizenship critically "with some notion of the value of evidence, some notion of relevance and irrelevance, and some discrimination between facts and prejudices" (p. 88–89). The committee went so far as to argue that students could not fulfill their civic responsibilities with a "skeptical" orientation toward citizenship.

In 1993, in response to fears that citizenship was not being treated sufficiently, Ontario introduced a distinct Grade 10 compulsory civics course. This civics course is housed within History and Geography curricula. These documents set objectives related to the abilities to "focus, organize, locate, record, evaluate/assess, synthesize/conclude, apply and communicate" (Ontario Ministry of Education, 1993, p. 6).

This new orientation toward citizenship education was meant to help students understand significant ongoing demographic changes. Students were encouraged to examine the "role that diverse cultures have played and continue to play within our country" (Ontario Ministry of Education, 1993, p. 7). There was explicit criticism of the way in which previous approaches to citizenship have emphasized "the values, experiences, achievements, and perspectives of white-European members of society" and have excluded or distorted "those of other groups in Canada and throughout the world" (Ontario Ministry of Education, 1993, p. 13). The document even went so far as to define a good citizen as one who values "the contributions of people from a variety of cultures, races, religions, socio-economic backgrounds, and abilities, in the school, community, Canada, and the world" (Ontario Ministry of Education, 1993, p. 23).

There have been several revisions to these Ministry of Education documents. The essential curricular content, now housed with History and Geography in what is known as Canadian and World Studies (Ontario Ministry of Education, 2015), remains the same. However, this most recent revision calls for an "inquiry-based approach" that encourages hands-on activities and is centered on a "self/spirit" model that stresses the need to take into account individual student health (cognitive, emotional, physical, and social). Citizenship education is also to be fostered through compulsory service programs in which students acquired graduation credits based on volunteer activity.

Running parallel to these programs and curriculum documents is a 2008 Ministry of Education initiative known as "character education," described as "the deliberate effort to nurture the universal attributes upon which schools and communities find consensus … They bind us together across the lines that often divide us in society." (Ontario Ministry of Education, 2008, p. 1).

So, in Ontario there has been a recent curricular shift away from static notions of nationalism based on fixed and stratified political hierarchies to more pluralistic and multidimensional orientations.

History of Citizenship Education in Quebec

The pattern of Quebec's citizenship education follows three historical periods. The first period, from 1875 to 1960, is known as the traditional era (Magnuson, 1987). It was marked by the 1875 Act which gave formal recognition to a dual denominational school system under the auspices of Catholic and Protestant leadership, and established a de facto dual French and English system with competing views of Canadian national history. The second, from the 1960s to the 1990s, coincided with the Quebec Quiet Revolution and the consolidation and centralization of Catholic and Protestant (and French and English) curricula under a single provincial educational policy objective. The third, from the 1990s to the present day, represents the notable rise of citizenship education as a defining feature of the new Quebec history curriculum.

A provincial model of education for Quebec had been in development since before Confederation, but it had always been characterized by an uneasy relationship between Catholics and Protestants, or French and English, who, by legislating the existence of "dissentient schools" in 1841—a provision that was carried into the BNA Act of 1867—created a dual system of education in the province. As a single provincial system was untenable, Quebec legislators chose to formally divide the system between Catholic and Protestant systems in 1875.

Catholics and Protestants, with separate schools, boards, and teacher training programs, did little to create a common curriculum. Similar to the rest of Canada, citizenship education in Quebec prior to the 1960s was contained in school history courses. What distinguished Quebec from the rest of Canada, however, is that its two school populations were themselves receiving two different levels of understanding about Canadian history. The pattern of history teaching in Protestant Quebec tended to be similar to that of English Canada, with links to a Canadian national narrative, while that of Catholic Quebec was steeped in another nationalistic narrative that "sang the praises of the trinity of family, church, and land" as it was manifested in Quebec (Éthier & Lefrançois, 2012, p. 23). In either case, students were not acquiring a civic education that had much connection to the world in which they lived (Hodgetts, 1968, p. 32).

The 1960s marked a profound change in Quebec education. When Jean Lesage's Liberal government came to office in 1960, it made education one of its top priorities, setting up a Royal Commission of Inquiry on Education. The commission's report essentially made the state the major player in education. The centralization of education brought with it a centralized project of curricular reform. While the teaching of history and civics initially faced a setback, with no compulsory history program in place from 1969 to 1974, social unrest in the early years of the 1970s convinced the Quebec government to implement a compulsory history course for all students as a means to civic harmony (Éthier & Lefrançois, 2012).

The history curriculum was once again revamped in 1982 and 1984, with a progressive emphasis on the new social history of the late twentieth century. With no stand-alone citizenship education or civics course, the irony of the new progressive social history was that its dethroning of political history also brought with it a diminished emphasis on issues of politics, governance, and other related topics essential for the teaching of citizenship education.

By the late 1990s, however, appetite for curricular reform grew again and the Quebec government revised the entire program. The designers of the new provincial curriculum explicitly made citizenship education a defining feature of Quebec education, linking it with the history curriculum (Quebec, 1997, 2001, 2004, 2007). A concerted effort to integrate the topics and ideas of citizenship education—including democracy, liberty, the nation, the state, and social activism—with the other core subjects of daily learning was made. Citizenship education as a concept, however, remains ubiquitously vague and no explanation of what citizenship is or how it might be defined is woven into the official curriculum. Nor is there any concrete pedagogy attached to it. It remains, at best, an extension of history education. Indeed, as Éthier, Lefrançois, and Demers have pointed out, the official title of the program itself—History and Citizenship Education—"eloquently demonstrates the extent and central importance of the mandate given, first and foremost, to history teachers" (Éthier, Lefrançois, & Demers, 2013, p. 120).

Citizenship Education Research in Canada Today

A review of more than 200 Canadian articles on citizenship education found that very few empirical studies have been conducted with Canadian youth. Citizenship education research can be divided into the following subtopics: (a) conceptual discussions exploring what citizenship education is largely framed within a post-modern, critical studies orientation. Scholars have critiqued how citizenship education often remains focused on creating "good citizens," in the sense of individuals who vote within a racialized, gendered, and classed society. They have questioned how the subject can be made more socially just; (b) citizenship education and its relations to school district policies particularly the perceived damaging effects of neoliberal discourse; (c) historical studies of citizenship education; (d) citizenship education in relation to multiculturalism, diversity, and pluralism, human rights education, values and social justice;

(e) international comparisons between Canada and other nations; (f) discussions of global citizenship education; (g) citizenship education teaching recommendations such as democratic classrooms, critical thinking, issues, or community-based instruction; and (h) a limited amount of work exploring student and teachers' views in some regions of Canada. This chapter adds to this work by conducting a survey study with Canadian youth in three provinces.

RESEARCH STUDY: METHODS AND DATA SOURCES

The conceptual model of youth civic behavior described in Chap. 1 was used as the basis for the development of the survey tool. University students in varied programs were invited to participate in the study in the Fall of 2015. Participants filled out the survey anonymously online. Participants entered their names in a draw for a $100 gift certificate. Youth were also invited to share their thoughts in more depth through interviews; however, the majority of participants declined to be interviewed.

LIMITATIONS OF STUDY FINDINGS

The researchers hoped to carry out data collection with youth across in Canada in varied socio-economic categories and varied post-secondary educational programs and careers. However, despite invitations to youth advertised in local online magazines and requests to colleges to participate in the study, youth participation remained limited primarily to university youth at three universities: the University of British Columbia in BC, Bishop's University in Quebec, and the University of Ottawa in Ontario. The findings give us a glimpse of what university youth may feel and do in relation to Canadian civic life and do not represent the scope of youth perceptions and actions in the nation, which can be the subject of future research.

SUMMARY OF RESEARCH FINDINGS: CANADA

Of the 157 youth who participated in the survey, the majority (63%) were female, reflecting a national trend to increased feminization of Canadian universities (see Table 2.1).

Most (59%) identified themselves as being "middle class" and as having Canadian (26%), French/French Canadian (18%), or European (44%) backgrounds and as being Canadian citizens (83%). Unlike the pilot study and national trends, few self-identified Ethnic minorities participated in

Table 2.1 Summary of Canadian findings (Data are in percentages)

Canadian Youth	Number of participants: 157		
Demographics			
Gender	Male: 37%	Female: 63%	Other/undisclosed: 0%
Citizenship/ nationality	Canadian: 83%	European: 8%	Other: 9%
First language	English: 62%	French: 24%	Other: 15%
Class	Upper: 12%	Middle: 60%	Other: 28%
	Yes	No	Do not remember
Citizenship education	64%	29%	6%
	Some knowledge		Lack knowledge
Political knowledge	68%		33%
	Yes	No	Unsure
Follow the news	77%	23%	
Personal political experience	39%	61%	1%
Family's political involvement	74%	26%	
Personality type	Assertive	Amiable	Humanistic	Analytical
	33%	37%	8%	17%
	Important		Not important
Attitude to community engagement	99%		1%
Attitude to political participation	71%		30%
	Effective		Ineffective
Level of personal efficacy	88%		12%
	Active	Somewhat active	Inactive
Civic involvement	16%	68%	16%
	Supportive	Neutral	Do not care/not supportive
Attitudes toward democracy	62%	30%	8%
Attitude toward govt. system in Canada	46%	46%	9%

(*continued*)

Table 2.1 (continued)

Canadian Youth	Number of participants: 157

Students' activities (Top 3)	Students' civic activities (Top 3)
Time with friends (96% of respondents said yes)	Voting (83%)
Interacting with social media (89%)	Being a good neighbor (82%)
Pop culture/going out for dinner (87%)	Volunteering (68%)

Granting citizenship (Top three)	To pay taxes (83% of respondents)
	To be interested in the common wellbeing (82%)
	To be a good neighbor (67%)

Crosstabs

Internal:

Personality-voting	No significant correlation
Personality-help people in need	Significant correlation, X^2 (4, $N = 157$) = 11.2, $p = .02$
Personality-donating money	Significant correlation, X^2 (4, $N = 157$) = 9.45, $p = .05$
Attitude: participation-active	Significant correlation, X^2 (2, $N = 157$) = 6.13, $p = .04$
Attitude: Canada-Voting	Significant correlation, X^2 (2, $N = 151$) = 7.96, $p = .01$
Self-efficacy-voting	Significant correlation, X^2 (1, $N = 152$) = 6.83, $p = .009$

External:

Knowledge-voting	Significant correlation, X^2 (1, $N = 157$) = 17.37, $p = .000$
Education-voting	Significant correlation, X^2 (2, $N = 157$) = 11.5, $p = .003$
Active family-voting	Significant correlation, X^2 (1, $N = 156$) = 8.68, $p = .003$
Political experience-voting	Significant correlation, X^2 (2, $N = 155$) = 11.9, $p = .003$
Citizenship-voting	Significant correlation, X^2 (7, $N = 156$) = 18.3, $p = .01$
Culture-attitude to Canada	Significant correlation, X^2 (16, $N = 141$) = 28.46, $p = .03$

the study (only about 12% of responses, with Ethnicities identified as Asian, East Asian, Latin American, African, or Middle Eastern). Most spoke English as their first language (62%), followed by French (24%). Most participants were between the ages of 18 and 28.

Most participants (64%) stated that they had taken citizenship education in school, and more than half (52%) felt it was important. However, some youth wrote comments that they did not enjoy their citizenship education, or that it was incomplete, difficult to understand, or not taught in the best way for them:

Useful content but wrong approach to teaching it (not engaging). (student #83)

It was insufficient; not enough practical info on political involvement. (student #102)

I did but not sufficient enough to make me understand how thing actually works. It was just a compilation of data. (student #118)

It could have been taught better (e.g. with a little more enthusiasm) but I still think it has been very useful and in fact critically important for me to learn, as a citizen of a democratic society. (student #128)

Teachers explained their opinions more than the actual facts. (student #3)

Some commented that it focused on teaching voting:

Understanding voting was useful yet more could be done on political party ideologies and current events. (student #126)

Most (68%) felt that they were knowledgeable or had some knowledge of government, although the majority (61%) stated they had not had a significant political experience. Those who had described experiences regarding tuition, refugees in Canada, discrimination and increasingly intolerance to Muslims and the Niqab issue, budget cut backs, healthcare issues, the environment and pipeline, or the silencing of researchers, all related to Conservative policies. Some mentioned Quebec separatism or stated that they did not trust politicians or believe these cared about youth:

Mostly I have little trust in the political jostling I hear about all the time. It seems like things get said to influence election results, but then what happens is not what was talked about. (student #78)

I am from Montreal so watching the Charbeneau commission and seeing all the illegal activities going on has skewed my perspective. (student #64)

I came to understand that politics has changed into a game with one particular group of people involved. Government is no longer for all the people because politicians put their personal interest first before they hear people concerns. (student #55)

A large majority (77%) followed the news, mostly online, due to their "personal interest" and desire to "be informed":

to keep up with what is happening in the world. (student #43)

I like to know whats (sic) going on around the world, it interests me. (student #76)

The majority (74%) stated that their parents were active politically, largely by talking about political issues or voting:

They keep up with the political news and vote every election. (student #25)

Most (43%) identified their parents as being Liberal in ideology, followed by Conservative and New Democratic Party (NDP)/Left last. The majority (48%) also identified themselves as Liberal in ideology, followed by NDP/Left and Conservative/Right last.

The youth selected varied personality types, with the most frequent being leader/assertive (33%) and amiable/friendly (37%), followed by introverted, humanist, and mixed types. They identified their top free time activities as spending time with friends (96% of participants), interacting with social media (89%), following pop culture and going out for dinner (87%), watching TV (82%), watching or playing sports (70%), and shopping/going to the Mall (70%). Few youth stated they participated in political (22%), patriotic (19%), or religious (19%) activities.

Most youth (99%) felt that it was important for people to be active in their communities. A majority (71%) also felt it was important for people to participate politically. Many (68%) also stated that they were occasionally active, and most (88%) felt they could be effective in their actions, thus demonstrating a high sense of self-efficacy. They stated that individuals, or groups of individuals, could have an effect on society, that people could make changes, and that it was important for people to be active in a democracy:

Because we do have an impact, but when we are many we will have an even greater one. Saying I won't make a difference is not true because if everyone were to do that then nobody would change anything. (student #34)

because Canada is a democratic nation and we are able to affect change by voting for different partys (sic). (student #64)

If I want to live in a world/community that I like I have to contribute to making that way instead of complaining about how it is. (student #123)

It is important for people to participate in order to make Canada a better place. (student #11)

Limitations on youth's active participation were associated with not valuing the process, prioritizing their time or actions, or not feeling part of the community:

> Student life means little time but its still important. (student #91)

> I don't involve myself in civic process or community events because I don't have a great sense of belonging to communities I live in or feel I have deep roots in any place. (student #135)

> I vote, try to be engaged with the present issues and participate to try to contribute to issues that I feel strongly about. (student #150)

While most were active to some event, however, they were active in primarily "traditional" political and civic activities: voting (83% of respondents), being a good neighbor (82%), volunteering (69%), helping those in need (61%), donating money to causes (55%), and following political news (48%). Few participated in political events (22%), boycotted (19%), protested (14%), joined civic groups (10%), joined a political party (6%), or wrote letters or news articles (5%). While the majority (62%) were supportive of democratic governments in general, less (46%) were supportive of the Canadian government (46% were neutral). It seems that these youth felt a need for a change in the government. In their comments on what their ideal government system would look like, youth wanted governments that listened to the people, were concerned about social and economic equality, reflected Canada's diversity, and worked to improve the nation and not in their own self-interests:

> A government made up of a coalition of peers, from all backgrounds and ethnic groups in Canada. (student #118)

> An ideal government would be one that works for the benefit of society and well being for ALL people by providing basic needs like food, water, shelter, education, and health programs. Power and money wouldn't be of importance. (student #122)

Reflecting their pluralistic nation and the emphasis placed on Canada as a multicultural nation, most youth stated that citizenship should be given to those who pay taxes, are interested in the common wellbeing, and are good neighbors. While most did feel that citizens should know the history and laws of the country, most did not feel that citizens had to share the same lifestyle, religion, or customs of the majority.

Thus, the findings show that the majority of participants were Canadians with European backgrounds, fluent in English and French. Most valued knowing the news and participation in civic and political life, and most were active to an extent, primarily in traditional civic or political activities.

CROSS-TABS ANALYSIS

In Chap. 1, we presented a model of youth civic engagement, arguing that youth engagement can be understood as the product of the interaction of internal and external factors. We explore the relations between internal and external factors and civic attitudes and behavior through cross-tabs analysis.

Internal Factors

We considered how features such as personality, gender, and attitudes may influence civic behavior and attitudes. We found no significant correlations between gender and voting behavior or self-identified class and voting. We also found no significant correlation between personality and voting, although we did find differences in other civic behaviors. That is, how youth labeled their personality affected their behaviors of helping those in need in the community. Those who identified themselves as amiable/ friendly or humanist personality types were more likely to donate money to causes, and those who identified themselves as amiable/friendly were more likely to help those in need, supporting findings from other research studies in this area (Dinesen, Norgaard, & Klemmensen, 2014; Metzger & Smetana, 2010; Omoto, Snyder, & Hackett, 2010). We also found significant correlations between attitudes and behaviors: those youth who stated that it was important for people to participate politically in Canada and those who were "supportive" of the Canadian government were also more actively involved. Finally, there was a strong correlation between having a sense of self-efficacy and behavior: those who felt that their actions could make a difference voted more than those who did not, also supporting previous research (Bandura, 1997; Beaumont, 2010).

External Factors

External factors also influenced youth's civic attitudes and behaviors. Youth who stated they had some knowledge of government processes and that they had studied citizenship education in school were more likely to vote. Family also influenced behavior, as youth who stated that their parents were civically active (primarily by voting or reading the news) were also more likely to vote. Youth who had had a significant experience were also more likely to vote. The number of responses from varied ethnic backgrounds was too small to carry out a good analysis between cultural background and civic behavior, although significant correlations were found, unsurprisingly, between identifying oneself as a Canadian and voting. There was also a relation between having a European background and having a more positive view of the Canadian government, with those from other backgrounds having a more neutral stance. There was no statistically significant relation between cultural background and sense of self-efficacy, the family's level of active involvement, or youth's knowledge of government.

Thus, the research identified connections between internal factors such as personality, attitude, and sense of self-efficacy and civic attitudes and behaviors, and between external factors and conditions such as school, family and experiences, and civic attitudes and behaviors.

DISCUSSION

Scholars have decried youth civic apathy (Gidengil, Blais, Nevitte, & Nadeau, 2004; Howe, 2010). However, this study, primarily with young Canadians at three universities, found that youth had a high sense of self-efficacy and that they participated in "traditional" forms of civic participation by voting in large numbers in the last election. Why did they vote? Youth were, along with many other Canadians, ready for a change in government. As largely middle class youth who identified with the Liberals and, particularly with the young Justin Trudeau who campaigned on positive change, more jobs, increased infrastructure spending, and the legalization of marijuana, youth were motivated to vote. Most probably, the Trudeau name—associated with Canada's Charter of Rights and Freedoms and Multiculturalism and the long governance of Justin Trudeau's father, which is often positively portrayed in school texts—also played a role in youth voting perceptions. Many youth were turned also off by the dark and scare tactics used by the Conservatives in their "attack" ads.

In the pilot study (Broom, 2016), youth did not identify themselves as having such a high sense of self-efficacy. It seems that the chance to vote and voting, along with the overwhelming electoral victory of Trudeau, went hand-in-hand with an increased sense of self-efficacy.

A number of factors enabled a strong youth vote. Most Canadian provinces have mandatory citizenship education programs, and these programs give attention to voting as a civic duty. Elections Canada, the national elections office, actively promotes education about voting in schools and provides numerous free resources. For the first time, election polls were placed on university campuses so that youth could vote at universities easily (Levinson King, 2015). Further, the survey findings found statistically significant correlations between citizenship education, knowledge of democracy, and family backgrounds and active participation through voting.

Thus, youth can get actively involved in voting and volunteering when they are motivated to do so. However, the findings demonstrated that Canadian youth have a traditional and limited, if inclusionary, conception of the behaviors of a citizen: citizens vote, pay their taxes, listen to the news, and participate in their communities through voting or donating money. These are a combination of Marshall's (1950) social and political conceptions of citizenship. Youth, largely, do not participate in more active or transformative citizenship processes (Evans, 2004), such as joining civic groups, boycotting, or writing to their MPs or newspapers. According to youth, citizens do not need to be born in the nation, but they do need to be "nice" people or good neighbors. Youth do not demonstrate the same contested, conflicting, and diverse conceptions of citizenship found in academic work. These youth, further, as youth attending universities where they are given access to training for professional careers, may not be representative of all Canadian youth. For instance, native youth may find it challenging to identify with a colonial government that has negatively affected their communities (Tupper, 2012). Indeed, the only native Canadian youth to fill out the survey identified himself as "working class," stated that he did not care about the Canadian government, that he was not active, and that "Stephen Harper doesn't care about Aboriginals" (Student response #107).

Time will tell whether Trudeau can fulfill his election promises and bring stability and increased job prospects for youth. Strong global pressures may influence Trudeau's ability to do so. Canada's economy has already begun to suffer in 2016 due to global economic forces such as the falling price of oil and devaluations in the Canadian dollar, and some provinces such as Alberta are facing increased unemployment. If Trudeau fails his mandate, youth perceptions about their self-efficacy and democracy may change again, thus illustrating challenges with representative democracy today and the fluid nature of citizenship attitudes and actions.

Youth also largely supported the legalization of the drug marijuana. What are the consequences of legalizing a drug that can lead to addiction and loss of motivation? The government's acceptance of a social trend in thought demonstrates how democratic government in some ways comes to reflect the changing social beliefs of its citizens. Democracy is a shell that mirrors its people in their moral makeup and mindset and, thus, determines the "culture" of citizenship in a nation.

CONCLUSION

This research study supported the conceptual model described in Chap. 1: youth behaviors are complex, influenced by individuals' socio-cultural and family backgrounds, individuals' personalities, and individuals' lived experiences. The study found that youth, at least some university youth, can be (or are) motivated to participate in traditional political and social citizenship processes, and that this is connected to citizenship education, knowledge of government and its processes, political experiences, and family backgrounds. Further, internal factors such as personality and attitude influence youth views and actions. Questions remain, however, about how youth in varied socio-economic circumstances feel and act.

EDUCATIONAL RECOMMENDATIONS

Citizenship education in schools works to some extent. Youth who remember taking citizenship education in schools and who identified themselves as having more knowledge of government were more active politically. Thus, schools should continue to teach citizenship education. However, youth continue to have traditional and limited views of what citizenship means, and youth stated that their citizenship education was limited to learning primarily about voting, or was boring or incomplete. Citizenship education in schools can be updated and revised to include more engaging methods such as experiential and inquiry-based learning, and engagement with and through social media.

Youth often chose voting or volunteering as the main behavior for a citizen (the "dutiful citizen conception" [Bennett, Freelon, & Wells, 2010]). Further investigations can occur as to which are the conceptions that the majority of teachers and textbooks teach, and university teacher education programs can give more attention to citizenship education. Curricula can include discussions of varied ways to participate, beyond voting and volunteering, and engage students in discussions on community issues. "Complicated conversations" (Pinar, 2004) about what citizenship is should be included. This requires that we consider what the "common" good is and entails (Broom, 2010) and that Canadian adults, teachers, and politicians look at their own actions. Youth are quite aware of the actions of the adults in their communities, and these are not always good examples of positive civic behaviors.

Youth voted for Trudeau based on his name and his election promises, not his past record. Possibly, youth's citizenship education programs may have influenced their perceptions by positively describing Trudeau's father's role in developing Canada's Charter of Rights and Freedoms and policy of multiculturalism. Youth may also have voted partly "in reaction" to a long Conservative term and a prime minister who some felt had become too Right wing. The leader of the NDP (a left/labor party), Mulcair, a quiet experienced leader, and his party were also decimated in the polls. Was Trudeau the right choice? Why did youth support the legalization of a drug? Citizenship education should include critical thinking education that has students explore what they believe, why they believe it, and what the implications of these beliefs are for the future of the nation. Civic education materials can help youth understand civic issues and empower them through a combination of knowledge, active and critical inquiry, and active engagement.

Finally, as active civic experience was statistically connected to civic involvement, authentic school–community partnerships can engage students in successfully collaborating on addressing local needs and issues in ways that help to promote thoughtful long-term engagement and empowerment.

REFERENCES

Bandura, A. (1997). *Self-efficacy: The exercise of control.* New York: Freeman.

Beaumont, E. (2010). Political agency and empowerment: Pathways for developing a sense of political efficacy in young adults. In L. Sherrod, J. Torney-Purta, & C. Flanagan (Eds.), *Handbook of research on civic engagement* (pp. 525–558). Hoboken, NJ: John Wiley & Sons.

Bennett, W., Freelon, D., & Wells, C. (2010). Changing citizen identity and the rise of a participatory media culture. In L. Sherrod, J. Torney-Purta, & C. Flanagan (Eds.), *Handbook of research on civic engagement* (pp. 393–423). Hoboken, NJ: John Wiley & Sons.

Broom, C. (2008). Change and continuity: A historical study of citizenship education in British Columbian social studies guides, 1930–2006. In D. K. et al. (Eds.), *Learning democracy by doing alternative practices in citizenship learning and participatory democracy* (pp. 98–110). Toronto, ON: TLC: University of Toronto.

Broom, C. (2010). Conceptualizing and teaching citizenship as humanity. *Citizenship Social and Economics Education, 9*(3), 147–155.

Broom, C. (2011). Change and continuity in British Columbian perspectives as illustrated in social studies textbooks, 1885–2006. *The Journal of Educational Media, Memory and Society, 3*(2), 42–57.

Broom, C. (2013). Social justice 12: Negotiating issues in and for a democratic society. *Social Studies Research and Practice, 8*(2), 68–82.

Broom, C. (2016). Exploring youth civic engagement and disengagement in British Columbia, Canada. *Journal of International Social Studies. 6(1)*, 4–22.

Broom, C., & Evans, R. (2015). Social Studies within and across borders. *Citizenship Education Research Journal, 4*(1), 56–69.

Bruno Joffre, R. (1998). *Manitoba history: Citizenship and schooling in Manitoba, 1918–1945*. Retrieved from http://www.mhs.mb.ca/docs/mb_history/36/citizenship.shtml.

Clarke, P. (2004). The historical contexts of social studies in English Canada. In A. Sears & I. Wright (Eds.), *Challenges and prospect for Canadian social studies* (pp. 17–37). Vancouver, BC: Pacific Educational Press.

Cordasco, F. (1976). *A brief history of education*. Totowa, NJ: Littlefield, Adams, and Co.

Curtis, B. (1988). *Building the educational state: Canada West, 1836–1871*. London, ON: The Althouse Press.

Dewey, J. (1938). *Experience and education*. New York: Touchstone.

Dinesen, P., Norgaard, A., & Klemmensen, R. (2014). The civic personality: Personality and democratic citizenship. *Political Studies, 62*(1), 134–152.

Éthier, M., & Lefrançois, D. (2012). How should citizenship be integrated into high school history programs? Public controversies and the Québec *History and Citizenship Education* curriculum: An analysis. *Canadian Social Studies, 45*(1), 21–42.

Éthier, M., Lefrançois, A., & Demers, S. (2013). An analysis of historical agency in Québec history textbooks. *Education, Citizenship, and Social Justice, 8*(2), 119–133.

Evans, R. (2004). *The social studies wars*. New York: Teachers' College.

Francis, D. (1997). *National dreams: Myth, memory and Canadian history*. Vancouver, BC: Arsenal Pulp Press.

Gidengil, E., Blais, A., Nevitte, N., & Nadeau, R. (2004). *Citizens*. Vancouver, BC: UBC Press.

Hébert, Y.M. (Ed.) (2002). *Citizenship in transformation in Canada*. Toronto: University of Toronto Press.

Hodgetts, A. B. (1968). *What culture? What heritage? A study of civic education in Canada*. Toronto, ON: OISE Press.

Howe, P. (2010). *Citizens adrift: The democratic disengagement of young Canadians*. Vancouver, BC: UBC Press.

Jenkins, R. (1918). *Canadian civics: BC edition*. Toronto, ON: Copp Clark Ltd.

Jorgensen, C. (2012). *John Dewey and the dawn of social studies: Unraveling conflicting interpretations of the 1916 report.* Charlotte, NC: IAP.

Levinson King, R. (2015). *Justin Trudeau got help from youth, new voters and social media in election win.* Retrieved from www.thestar.com

MacLean, M. (2012). *Shifts shaking Canadian youth, says report from Community Foundations of Canada.* Retrieved from http://communityfoundations.ca/generation-flux-seismic-shifts-shaking-canadian-youth-says-report-from-community-foundations-of-canada/

Magnuson, R. (1987). The public school myth, Quebec education 1875–1960. *McGill Journal of Education, 22*(1), 28–40.

Marshall, T. H. (1950). *Citizenship and social class and other essays.* Cambridge: Cambridge University Press.

Metzger, A., & Smetana, J. (2010). Social cognitive development and adolescent civic engagement. In L. Sherrod, J. Torney-Purta, & C. Flanagan (Eds.), *Handbook of research on civic engagement* (pp. 221–248). Hoboken, NJ: John Wiley & Sons.

Ministry of Education, British Columbia (1997). *Social studies 11 integrated resource package.* Victoria, BC: Province of British Columbia, Ministry of Education.

Ministry of Education, British Columbia (2005). *Social studies 11 integrated resource package.* Victoria, BC: Province of British Columbia.

Morrison, J. (2013). *The top five challenges facing Millenials in Canada.* Retrieved from http://abacusinsider.com/canadian-millennials/top-5-challenges-facing-millennials-canada-millennials/#sthash.KgBNvsBa.dpu

Omoto, A., Snyder, M., & Hackett, J. (2010). Personality and motivational antecedents of activism and civic engagement. *Journal of Personality, 78*(6), 1703–1734.

Ontario Ministry of Education (1993). *The common curriculum.* Toronto, ON: Author.

Ontario Ministry of Education (2008). *Finding common ground: Character development in Ontario schools, K-12.* Toronto, ON: Author.

Ontario Ministry of Education (2015). *Canadian and world studies, 2015 (revised).* Toronto, ON: Author.

Ontario Ministry of Education Social Sciences Study Committee (1962). In N. Frye (Ed.), *Design for learning: Report* (pp. 88–89). Toronto: University of Toronto Press.

Osborne, K. (1996). Education is the best national insurance: Citizenship education in Canadian schools, past and present. *Canadian and International Education, 25*(2), 33–58.

Patrias, C. (2006). Socialists, Jews, and the 1947 Saskatchewan Bill of Rights'. *The Canadian Historical Review, 87*(2), 265–292.

Pinar, W. (2004). *What is curriculum theory?* Mahwah, NJ: L. Erlbaum Associates.

Quebec (1997). *Réaffirmer l'école, rapport du Groupe de travail sur la réforme du curriculum d'études du primaire et du secondaire*. Québec: Ministère de l'Éducation.

Quebec (2001). *Québec education program: Preschool education, elementary education*. Québec: Ministère de l'Éducation.

Quebec (2004). *Québec education program: Secondary school education, cycle one*. Québec: Ministère de l'Éducation du Loisir et du Sport.

Quebec (2007). *Québec education program: Secondary school education, cycle two*. Québec: Ministère de l'Éducation du Loisir et du Sport.

Russell, R. (2002). Bridging the boundaries for a more inclusive citizenship education. In Y. Hebert (Ed.), *Citizenship in transformation in Canada* (pp. 134–149). Toronto: University of Tornoto.

Sears, A., & Hughes, A. (1996). Citizenship education and current educational reform. *Canadian Journal of Education, 21*(2), 123–142.

Seixas, P. (Ed.) (2004). *Theorizing historical consciousness*. Toronto: University of Toronto Press.

Tomkins, G. (1986). *A common countenance: Stability and change in the Canadian curriculum*. Scarborough, ON: Prentice-Hall.

Troper, H. (2002). The historical context for citizenship education in Urban Canada. In Y. Hebert (Ed.), *Citizenship in transformation in Canada* (pp. 150–161). Toronto, ON: University of Tornoto.

Tupper, J. (2012). Treaty education for ethically engaged citizenship: Settler identities, historical consciousness and the need for reconciliation. *Citizenship Teaching & Learning, 7*(2), 143–156.

Wertsch, J. (2002). *Voices of collective remembering*. Cambridge: Cambridge University Press.

CHAPTER 3

Exploring Youth Civic Engagement: A View from England

Richard Harris

Citizenship, as a school subject, in England has had a chequered and difficult history; it has never traditionally been taught as an explicit subject prior to 2000 (Kerr, 2005), and the attitude of the UK government has historically been very laissez-faire in terms of outlining any form of curriculum requirement. It was not until the 1988 Education Reform Act that a national curriculum in England was developed. This identified subjects that were to be 'core' and those that were to be 'foundation' ones. At this stage, citizenship was merely part of the 'basic curriculum,' included as one of a number of cross-curricular themes that were also to be covered.

It was not until the late 1990s that the New Labour government of Tony Blair took steps to change the status of citizenship. Following the Crick Report of 1998 (QCA, 1998), citizenship became a 'foundation' subject, which meant teaching it became statutory, with a compulsory programme of study (*DfEE/QCA*, 1999). The development was prompted by growing concerns over the social, moral and political fabric of society (Harris, 2006). The aim of the new curriculum was ambitious, striving for:

R. Harris (✉)
Institute of Education, University of Reading, Reading, UK
e-mail: r.j.harris@reading.ac.uk

© The Author(s) 2017   37
C. Broom (ed.), *Youth Civic Engagement in a Globalized World*,
Palgrave Studies in Global Citizenship Education and Democracy,
DOI 10.1057/978-1-137-56533-4_3

no less than a change in the political culture of this country …; for people to think of themselves as active citizens, willing, able and equipped to have an influence in public life and with the critical capacities to weigh evidence before speaking and acting; to build on and to extend radically to young people the best in existing traditions of community involvement and public service, and to make them individually confident in finding new forms of involvement and acting among themselves. (QCA, 1998)

Schools however faced numerous challenges implementing the new curriculum; for example, there were few subject specialists to teach it, it was supposed to occupy 5 % of an already crowded school timetable and there was confusion over the precise nature of the subject (Kerr, Cleaver, Ireland, & Blenkinsop, 2003; Ofsted, 2004, 2005).

The model of citizenship as outlined in the curriculum was heavily influenced by the thinking of T.H. Marshall; thus, the curriculum was underpinned by the ideas of developing young people's political literacy, social and moral responsibility and community involvement. It was however criticised on a number of fronts. Some have questioned whether it is a subject to be studied (Pring, 2006), whilst others attacked its commitment to the (essentially elitist) political status quo, (Faulks, 2006) and its narrow, nationalistic conception of citizenship (Faulks, 2006; Kiwan, 2008).

Subsequent reviews of the National Curriculum (*DfE*, 2013; QCA, 2007) have seen the statutory content of the citizenship curriculum altered. Following the review in 2007, the curriculum document focused on the concepts of democracy and justice, rights and responsibilities, identities and diversity, and the processes of critical thinking, advocacy and taking informed and responsible action. The biggest change here was the introduction of the idea of identity, with a focus on the idea of multiple identities. However, the curriculum review instigated by the Coalition government in 2010 seriously questioned the place of citizenship in the curriculum. The expert panel, which advised the government, recommended that citizenship revert back to being part of the basic curriculum (*DfE*, 2011).

However, the subject has retained its foundation status, but there has been a shift towards a knowledge-based curriculum, with a particular focus on knowledge of political systems, especially the UK's system of government and the 'precious liberties enjoyed by the citizens of the United Kingdom' (*DfE*, 2013). The consequences of this are yet to be fully seen, but Ofsted (2013) noted some schools have already started to pay less attention to the subject.

THE IMPACT OF CITIZENSHIP EDUCATION IN ENGLAND

Given the importance attached to the introduction of citizenship education, a large-scale longitudinal study was conducted by the National Foundation for Educational Research (NFER) from 2002–2010. Over 24,000 students from 169 schools were invited to complete questionnaires in 2002–2003, 2005, 2007 and 2009 as they progressed through school. An additional 2500 students were sent questionnaires biennially to capture views from other schools not involved in the longitudinal study, and interviews with staff and teachers were conducted in 12 schools every two years. In part, the study focused on how schools were implementing the new curriculum, but the reports from 2003 (Kerr et al.), 2006 (Ireland, Kerr, Lopes, Nelson & Cleaver), 2008 (Benton, Cleaver, Featherstone, Kerr, Lopes & Whitby) and 2010 (Keating, Kerr, Benton, Mundy & Lopes) focused heavily on the students' attitudes towards citizenship, community and participation, and provided rich insights into the thinking and experiences of this first generation of students to receive statutory education in citizenship.

Generally speaking, the study found that attitudes towards many issues were relatively stable, and that changes in attitudes were likely to be related to the age of the students rather than the impact of citizenship education per se (Keating et al., 2010, p. 61).

This is similar to a wider international study reported by Isac, Maslowski, Creemers, and van der Werf (2014), who found schooling had a negligible impact on students' civic knowledge, attitudes and behaviours. Few students showed any interest in political activity (beyond voting), being more inclined, if at all, to engage in civic activities such as fund raising and volunteering. This promoted Benton et al. (2008) to worry about a 'democratic deficit' amongst young people. The only area where there were signs of increased political engagement through the NFER project was within the school community, where students showed a strong commitment to their community and had more opportunities to participate in things like elections for school councils. Generally, students reported low levels of efficacy, persistently feeling an inability to bring about change, either within school, the local community or at a national level (Benton et al., 2008; Ireland et al., 2006; Kerr et al., 2003), It was also evident that students had a limited sense of what citizenship entailed. Invariably 'good' citizenship revolved around voting, being law-abiding and making a positive contribution to the local community.

These findings seem to reflect attitudes more widely; a large government survey (Home Office, 2004) revealed that only 38 % of adults felt they could influence decisions in their local area, which fell to 19 % when applied to the national scene, and although around 38 % of adults had engaged in some form of civic participation or informal volunteering in the previous 12 months, only 3 % did so on a monthly basis.

The Current Political Climate

Prior to the election of 2010, politics in the UK were dominated by New Labour under the premiership of Tony Blair, then Gordon Brown. The economic crisis saw a shift in the political landscape; in 2010, a Coalition government of the Conservative and Liberal Democrat parties was formed, a highly unusual situation in the UK.

These recent elections have been characterised by low turnouts—less than two thirds of the electorate voted (significantly lower than other elections since the end of World War Two), with only around 44 % of those aged 18–24 exercising their right to vote (UK Political Info, n.d.).

Explaining this decline in turnout is difficult. It could simply be apathy amongst the younger generation, but equally it could be disengagement as a response to the current political and economic climate. The period around 2009–2010 saw considerable public anger surrounding an expenses scandal involving MPs. Trust in the political system has been further shaken by the financial crisis of 2008 and subsequent economic downturn. Austerity measures introduced by the Coalition government have seen massive cuts in public spending. Youth unemployment has been stubbornly high. Those on low incomes have been badly hit by government policies, whilst tax cuts for those on higher incomes has helped to fuel a growing wage gap. Claims of tax avoidance, especially by large global corporations, such as Amazon, Google and Starbucks, also sparked widespread public anger. Taken together, these events have served to make different sections of the community feel disempowered and disconnected from the political system.

Major educational reforms have also affected those under 18 and have included an overhaul of the curriculum and examination system. Arguably, the most controversial change has been to university tuition fees; the Liberal Democrats had in particular pledged prior to the election to resist any increase in fees, but then supported a huge increase in annual fees, which rose from £3000 to £9000 for students.

The one issue that did positively capture the public imagination was the referendum on Scottish independence. This saw a massive turnout, with 85 % of the Scottish electorate voting (including those aged 16 and 17 who were allowed to vote on this issue).

The political landscape following the 2015 election changed in unexpected ways. The Conservative Party won an unexpected small majority (with the UK's 'first past the post' electoral system they were able to do this with 37 % of the vote). The Scottish Nationalist Party, given a major boost by the referendum campaign, won 56 out of the 59 seats in Scotland (having previously only had six seats). The Labour Party did badly, especially in Scotland, whilst the Liberal Democrat Party was virtually wiped out (having attracted a lot of criticism, especially over their position on tuition fees).

It was against this background of civic engagement that this study was conducted, with the intention of drawing upon international comparisons to see whether the issues identified in earlier studies continued to be seen in England and how this compared to young people in other nations.

EXPLORING YOUTH CIVIC ENGAGEMENT
AND DISENGAGEMENT IN ENGLAND

Students at a sixth form college in the south of England were invited to participate in an online survey. The area, according to the government's Income Deprivation Affecting Children Index (IDACI) data which are used to identify the socio-economic nature of an area, is ranked 17,310 out of 32,482 (with 1 being the most deprived area and 32,482 being the most affluent) therefore indicating this area is firmly in the middle ground regarding socio-economic status. Young people aged 16–19 attend the college, where the majority study for their A level examinations. Not all students in England attend a sixth form college, as most tend to study for their A levels in a school for students aged 11–18, but in this particular region, schools tend to take students aged 11–16, and students then choose from a number of sixth form colleges. This means that the students at this college come from a number of different schools within the area and so have different experiences of citizenship education from those schools.

The online survey site only allowed for a maximum of 150 responses, and this number was reached very shortly after the survey was opened. Details about the demographic profile are presented in Table 3.1. In terms of cultural affiliation, the majority chose British, but the remainder came from a range of African, Asian, European and Pacific nations. However, 87 %

Table 3.1   Summary of English participants' survey responses

Demographics of British youth in the survey

Gender	Female: 69 %[a] (104)	Male: 29 % (44)	Other: 1 % (2)
Age profile	16: 46 % (31)	17: 50 % (75)	18: 19 % (29)
Socio-economic status	'high': 4 % (6)	'middle': 77 % (115)	'low': 16 % (24)
Cultural identification	British: 67 % (101)	Other: 27 % (40)	Undisclosed: 6 % (9)
First language	English: 137 (91 %)	Other: 13 (9 %)	
Personality type	Leader: 47 % (37)	Friendly: 11 % (16) Outgoing: 22 % (33)	Introverted: 31 % (47)

Survey responses

	Yes	No	Unsure
Citizenship education about govt.	39 % (59)	53 % (79)	8 % (12)
	Knowledgeable	Some knowledge	Lack knowledge
Knowledge of govt. and politics	23 % (32)	63 % (88)	14 % (9)
	Yes	Sometimes	No
Follow the news	61 % (91)	37 % (55)	3 % (4)
	Yes	No	Unsure
Personal experience	22 % (32)	73 % (109)	5 % (8)
Family interest	17 % (25)	71 % (107)	5 % (8)
	Important	Quite important	Not important
Civic engagement	47 % (71)	47 % (70)	4 % (6)
	Active	Occasionally active	Not active
Level of personal engagement	21 % (32)	47 % (71)	27 % (40)
	Effective	Somewhat effective	Ineffective
Ability to influence change	25 % (35)	45 % (63)	31 % (43)
	Supportive	Neutral	Do not care/not supportive
Attitudes towards democracy	65 % (88)	22 % (30)	13 % (17)
Attitude towards govt. system in UK	39 % (55)	46 % (65)	14 % (20)
	Important	Neutral	Not important
Political engagement	54 % (75)	39 % (55)	7 % (10)

(*continued*)

Table 3.1   (continued)

Students' civic participation (top 3) (NB voting was 9th on the list; however, few of the students surveyed were of voting age)	Yes	No	No response
Donating money to causes	64 % (96)	33 % (50)	3 % (4)
Volunteering	61 % (91)	37 % (55)	3 % (4)
Being a good neighbour	51 % (77)	46 % (69)	3 % (4)

ªAll percentages are valid percentages, that is, reflects the number of actual responses to each question, and are rounded to the nearest whole number

(131) said their nationality was British. The majority of the sample identified their first language as English; other languages included Nepalese, Polish, Marathi, Italian, Hungarian, Mandarin, Spanish, Gujarati, Dutch, Tamil, and Tagalog.

Table 3.1 provides details of responses to many of the questions asked, which will be referred to as appropriate during the following discussion of the findings.

Citizenship Education

Although citizenship education has been compulsory in schools in England since 2002, so all the students should have been taught the subject, fewer than half said they had learned about government structures and processes at school, whereas the majority had either not studied it or could not remember (see Table 3.1). In one way, this is surprising as political literacy was part of the first curriculum and democracy was part of the revised 2007 curriculum; however, the Ofsted (2010) report, *Citizenship Established?* showed that where school provision was weak, it tended to be in the area of government and politics. In addition, one of the issues facing schools was how to find space in the curriculum for this new subject. Some schools taught it as a discrete subject, but the majority combined it with Personal, Social, Health and Economic education

(PSHE) and used non-specialist teachers, a model which has generally been associated with weaker outcomes for citizenship education (Keating, Kerr, Lopes, Featherstone, & Benton, 2009; Kerr et al., 2007; Ofsted, 2010) because students (and some teachers) are sometimes unclear as to the difference between PSHE and citizenship (essentially PSHE covers issues that fall within the personal sphere, whereas citizenship relates to the public sphere). So it is entirely possible that the way in which the curriculum has been presented to students has inhibited their knowledge and understanding of citizenship issues.

When asked whether they had found the material on government useful, only 51 students agreed it had been. Many students clearly had had a positive experience at school; in response to an open question about their experience of studying citizenship at school, 40 students spoke about how relevant they had found learning about citizenship or could identify why it was relevant. However, others had had a poorer experience; 10 students felt the lessons had been poorly taught, so they had failed to engage with the topics, whilst 21 responses explained that the lessons in school had lacked detail, leaving students with little insights into the political system. This lack of knowledge was evident in response to a direct question asking student to indicate how knowledgeable they felt about government and politics; only around a quarter said they were knowledgeable, with nearly two thirds claimed to have some knowledge, whilst the remainder felt they lacked any knowledge. This does beg the question where do students learn about political issues, and it seems from the survey that students gain their knowledge largely through the media.

Most students said they followed the news regularly, with many others doing so occasionally. The vast majority of respondents, nearly two thirds, were interested in global news issues, about one sixth were interested mainly in national issues and a couple focused more on local matters. Just over half obtained their news online, with TV being the next most favoured means, used by just over a third of the respondents. Print and radio was cited by hardly any students as a source of news.

Personal Experience of Political Matters

Relatively few students had personal experience of political matters, either directly or indirectly. Respondents were also invited to explain their answers further and detail their experience of political matters. Twenty-eight students responded. The issue most readily identified was education.

Eleven students were angry about changes to the education system introduced by the former Coalition government (formed by the Conservative
and Liberal Democrat parties), and in particular the large increase in university tuition fees, which would affect these students as they were studying courses that would allow them access to university. The following
comments illustrate the concerns raised:

> If I had to pick one area the government has control of which has affected
> me, it would be education. They need to consult students before making
> any major changes because at the end of the day we are the ones who are
> benefiting from it, not the government. (student #14)

> Nick Clegg [leader of the Liberal Democrats] promised to cut tuition fees
> in the 2010 election and he didn't. (student #150)

There were five comments about equality issues, mainly related to racism and Lesbian, Gay, Bisexual and Transgender (LGBT) issues, and five
comments about the political system, particularly distrust of politicians
(especially in the wake of the 'expenses scandal'). Three students expressed
concern over environmental issues, and the remainder covered individual
points. In all cases, the students focused on the way that political matters
had impinged on their lives or attitudes, rather than ways in which they had
engaged with the political system.

Students were also asked to provide open-ended responses to explain
their views relating to family engagement in political matters and 27 chose
to do so. Of these 11 indicated that their family's level of political activity
was restricted to voting. Only three responses showed any further degree
of political participation; one said their parents had signed petitions, one
had been involved with a protest over marriage equality (presumably gay
marriage rights given the timing of the survey, although this was not made
clear) and one had actively campaigned for a political party in the locality.

Civic Engagement

The students were asked to indicate how important it was for someone
to be actively involved in improving their communities, to which the
responses were overwhelmingly positive. Yet their personal levels of activity were much more limited. Only around half of those who said it was
important to be actively involved described themselves as active, whilst
over a quarter said they had no active engagement in civic matters. When
asked what types of civic activity they engaged with, the main responses

were donating money, volunteering, and being neighbourly. These are either relatively simple acts to engage with or are community based rather than political in nature.

Although many students felt civic engagement was important, few were active themselves and this may be linked to their sense of personal efficacy and the ability to influence change. As can be seen in Table 3.1, only a quarter of the respondents felt they could effectively influence change, whereas nearly a third thought they had no influence at all. Looking at the more detailed reasons why students felt this way, their comments demonstrated the youth to have a strong perception that individuals were powerless; 61 comments specifically focused on either the weakness of individuals to change things or stressed that only collective action could achieve anything.

> A small group of people can't make much of a difference you have to have a lot of people working together to get a proper impact. (student #8)

> Because the general public although have perceived control actually has very little control, government decides most of what happens whether that be regional or local—for example students didn't want exams to change but the government made a decision to change it. (student #43)

A further 14 responses also showed that the students felt that they were either too young, too unimportant or simply not trusted for their views to be taken seriously:

> I feel I'm too young to be taken seriously. (student #39)

> I'm a teenager. We are seen are vandals and hoodlums who have nothing but bad intentions. (student #42)

Although as the following response suggests, some young people feel they could make a positive difference if only they were listened to:

> If myself and other youth like me were to have the means and power to speak their mind in a way that would reach the whole community, I feel that a lot of social issues would finally be brought to light and addressed. In order for us to make a difference we need to be given that chance, and when given that opportunity I believe that we would make the most of it and make a positive change to society. (student #40)

Only 31 more detailed responses suggested that individuals could make, or at least make some, difference to society.

Anyone can make a difference, even alone. (student #71)

Because to make a real difference on a large scale it takes more than one person to speak up but locally sometimes it only takes one person. (student #104)

These findings support earlier studies, which show young people have low to moderate levels of efficacy in bringing about change (Benton et al., 2008; Keating et al., 2010).

Attitudes Towards Government and Democracy

The vast majority of students were positive about democracy per se, but less supportive of the UK system of government (see Table 3.1). The concerns expressed about the UK system were that it does not always fairly represent the views of the people:

Our system benefits the rich elites, ignoring the majority of the population. (student #41)

It's a good idea but most people are not represented. (student #50)

Democracy is a good concept, but when there are only 3 main parties people can choose from, all having similar plans for the country, it seems like there isn't really a choice in our democracy. (student #65)

As with levels of civic engagement, many students felt that it was important for them to be active in the political arena. Generally speaking, the responses to the open-ended question asking students to elaborate on their answer showed that they felt everyone's voice needed to be heard:

If you don't participate, you can't change things you don't like. (student #16)

If you don't use your voice, you can't complain if it's unheard. (student #137)

But there were signs of either cynicism or a lack of personal efficacy:

Sometimes I think it is worth speaking out but a lot of the time realistically voices don't get heard and nothing actually changes. (student #113)

At the end of the survey, students were invited to add any comments regarding any of the issues and some chose to write about their views on government, a number of which were heartfelt and showed an awareness of issues within society:

> The current system we have is clearly not working; it's designed to benefit the "ruling class" who are centred around greed. I don't know what the new system would look like or what it should look like. However I know it should not socialise the upcoming generations into becoming blinded, obedient slaves that use up their lives to line the pockets of the rich, it should not create vast economic disparity, it should not cause massive, irreversible damage to the environment all in the name of profit and it should provide everyone with a free and fulfilling life regardless of race, gender, sexuality or beliefs. I am only a 17 year old boy, and even I can see the problems within our society, so surely highly educated politicians can see it too. So why are, these people who are meant to represent us, not doing anything about it? (student #46)

Generally, the findings from this survey resonate with earlier studies. Nelson, Wade, and Kerr (2010) concluded that young people in England were broadly supportive of democracy and were willing to vote, but their level of interest in political issues and willingness to engage in political activity was much more limited. Lopes, Benton, and Cleaver's (2009) study suggested that young people's levels of engagement were largely dictated by perceived self-benefit from participation. Given the low levels of efficacy in bringing about change identified in the findings from the survey, it could be argued that these young people do not see they have much say in how things could change and therefore see little personal benefit from political engagement.

Perceptions of What Makes You a Citizen

The respondents were asked to identify particular attributes and actions which would be necessary conditions for being a citizen of their country. The most popular responses were:

- Paying taxes—83 % (although this was in the context of much media attention at the time about big corporations avoiding paying tax in the UK)
- Being interested in the common well-being—68 %
- Speaking the language of the country in which you live—60 %
- Being a good neighbour—50 %

- Knowing the history of the country and rules of government—43 %
- Being born in the country—29 %

These suggest that the students regard citizenship overwhelmingly in terms of what an individual can contribute to the community, and that they are expected to be caring and law-abiding. This fits very strongly into the idea of civil and social values, rather than defining it in political and legal terms. Interestingly, only two students chose sharing the same religion, whilst ten chose sharing the same lifestyle, which suggests that these young people are accepting of different lifestyles and belief systems, and do not see the need for others to accept a particular set of customs as a prerequisite for citizenship.

An open-ended comment box at the end of the survey allowed participants to elaborate more fully on some points. Some students were concerned that existing institutions in the UK should be respected and that loyalty to the UK should be a key aspect of citizenship:

> There should be an understanding between all cultures but I'm pretty against sharia law. The head of the UK is the monarch not religion and if they feel sharia law is the way to go then why come live in the UK? The British have their own law and regulation. Also the British citizenship should have that key question that asks "Would you fight for the UK" and if answered no they should fail the test instantly. If there is no attachment to UK then they are most likely here just for benefits and if shit hits the fan they will be the first to leave while I will gladly fight till the end. (student #135)

However, more responses stressed a positive view towards immigrants, but raised concerns about how people within the UK were being manipulated into more negative views towards them:

> I think there should be as little requirements as possible to get citizenship somewhere. Immigration should be actively encouraged—I think it is good for our economy, society, culture and wellbeing for it to be as diverse and varied as possible. Also, people shouldn't have limits on them where they can and can't live. As long as they pay the taxes for that country, then I think it is fine for them to live there. (student #9)

> The recent events that have taken place in the Middle East have heightened racial tensions. In the UK I have seen many scenarios of Islamophobia for example. Organisations such as UKIP (UK Independence Party), BNP (British National Party) and the EDL (English Defence League) have all

gained support because of this closed mindedness and lack of understanding and knowledge to be quite frank. Education is one of the best ways to fight this cultural change, yes, I do think this cultural change should be fought. Nationalism and patriotism are being used as excuses for closed mindedness and sometimes racism. Educate children on world affair, from all sorts of different views, ensure they are given many perspectives on current affairs. Teach them not to be easily persuaded by bias, teach them how to formulate independent views that take into considerations the situation from many angles. (student #30)

I feel that it is wrong to expect a person to 'share the same religion and lifestyle' as the country when our country is so diverse. It's unfair and prejudiced. There are also plenty of British citizens who are not 'good neighbours' or interested in the common wellbeing and not everyone knows the history of our country. Even less people know the rules of government. So I think it's unfair and elitist to expect this of people trying to get citizenship when a percentage of our own citizens can't fulfil these requirements. A basic, general understanding is of course necessary I think. (student #53)

Although only a few students commented on issues relating to immigration, the general responses regarding attributes and actions for people to be granted citizenship suggest a more tolerant and accepting position from the students who responded to this survey, which runs counter to findings in other studies. For example, Kerr (2005) and Nelson et al. (2010) found that pupils were broadly intolerant of immigration. Although further work would be needed to explore this issue further for a stronger claim to be made.

The Relationship between 'Internal' Factors and Civic Engagement

Overall analysis of the data did not reveal strong correlations between a range of internal factors and the levels of civic engagement, although some trends were discernible.

Knowledge of Politics and Government and Attitudes to Civic Engagement

Students' knowledge of politics and government did not reveal any statistically significant correlations, although there were some noticeable trends. Those who claimed to be knowledgeable about political issues were more likely to feel they could influence change. This was most noticeable when analysing whether the respondents felt they could **not** bring about change. Amongst those who felt knowledgeable, approximately 19 % felt as individuals they would be ineffective in bringing about change, for those who had some knowledge, the figure rose to 30 %, and for those with no knowledge, the figure was higher at 45 %.

Regarding support for democracy and the type of government in the UK, there was an inverse relationship between the level of support and degree of knowledge. Those with higher levels of knowledge were twice as likely to support the type of UK governmental system compared to those who said they lacked knowledge of the political system, and a similar pattern was discernible for democracy generally. When analysing how important it was to participate in civic activities, there was a similar trend as described above between the degree of knowledge and the perception that participation was important. A mixed picture was evident when respondents were asked about how actively engaged they were in a range of civic activities. The most active were those with **some** knowledge of political issues, with a quarter claiming to be active and nearly half saying they were occasionally active. Of those who claimed to be knowledgeable and of those with little knowledge, few were actively engaged in civic activities, but around half were occasionally involved.

Personality Type and Civic Behaviour

Previous studies (Dinesen, Nørgaard, & Klemmensen, 2014; Metzger & Smetana, 2010) had suggested that personality type has an influence over people's disposition towards civic participation. The findings from this study lend some support to this idea, but are not strong. Those in the 'leader' and 'friendly' categories were more likely to demonstrate civic behaviours, but the figures only account for 11 % of all responses.

Generally, those in the 'leader' category were more likely to be knowledgeable about politics (29 % said they were knowledgeable and 53 % said they had some knowledge), more likely to support the UK system of government (56 %) and feel they could influence change (31 % said they could, and 40 % said they would have some effect). Overall, they seem to have a higher sense of engagement with aspects of political activity, although in all cases, the figures are not statistically significant.

Those who identified as 'outgoing' were more likely to be engaged in community focused activity (63 % said it was important to be involved and 31 % said they were actively involved), but also recognised the importance of supporting democracy as a form of government (both generally—77 %—and in the UK—43 %).

Altogether, the four personality types were generally supportive of democracy, but support for the UK system of government was weakest amongst those who were 'introverted' (37 %) and 'friendly' (26 %). Those who felt least able to effect change were the 'friendly type' (16 %), and the level of engagement in the community was lowest amongst 'introverts' (12 %).

Gender

Comparing responses by gender shows some trends, but again revealed nothing statistically significant; males generally reported higher levels of political knowledge, whereas females were more likely to be involved in community issues; 43 % of males said they were knowledgeable and 45 % said they had some knowledge; for females, the figures were 16 % and 70 %, respectively. Both genders reported a similar sense of efficacy in bringing about change, although girls were slightly more positive; 48 % of girls felt they could be somewhat effective with 30 % saying they would not be able to influence change.

Females were also slightly more likely to feel it was important to be involved in improving the community and be more active; 52 % said it was important to be involved, compared to 42 % of males. Females were almost twice as likely to claim they were actively involved in the community, with 24 % claiming participation, compared to 14 % of males.

Sense of Efficacy

As noted above, students generally revealed a low sense of personal efficacy in terms of influencing events in the local community or society more broadly. Factors such as knowledge of the political system, personality type, gender and social class did not have much bearing on young people's sense of efficacy.

However, analysis relating involvement in civic activity did reveal a statistically significant relationship between the level of activity in civic processes and sense of personal efficacy ($p=.001$). What is not clear is how this relationship operates, that is, whether higher levels of self-efficacy lead individuals into civic activity or involvement in civic activity promotes higher levels of efficacy.

The Relationship between 'External' Factors and Civic Engagement

As with the internal factors no clear or strong correlations were found between young people's level of civic engagement and external factors, although there were evident trends.

School

It has been claimed that schools do influence the ways that students engage with citizenship and civic activities (Keating et al., 2010; Ofsted, 2010, 2013), and this study provides some evidence to support these. For example, those who remember being taught about politics and government were more likely to follow the news (70 %) compared to those who were not taught this in school (55 %) or could not remember being taught (58 %). Also students who had been taught about politics and government were more likely to be supportive of the UK system—48 % as opposed to 37 % of those who were not taught and 17 % of those who could not remember.

There was also a trend regarding levels of participation. Nearly 60 % of those who were taught about politics and government thought it was important for people to be actively involved in their community, and 65 % thought it was important to participate in civic activities. The corresponding figures for those who claim not to have been taught or could not remember being taught about politics were much lower.

This would suggest that education in school does have an effect on how students perceive the importance of participation, yet the actual levels of participation were low across all three types of response, with between 20 and 25 % saying they engaged in civic activities.

Family and Prior Political Encounters

It would be reasonable to assume that family influence and personal experience would shape young people's attitudes towards civic engagement. Although the data show there is a positive relationship between these factors, it does not appear to be a strong one.

A third of those who claimed to be knowledgeable about politics had families who were politically active (although as discussed previously this often does not extend beyond voting), which is reduced to a fifth where families were not active. However, there were some surprising results. Students whose families were not active in politics felt more strongly that they could be 'somewhat effective' in bringing around change compared to families considered active (45 % compared to 29 %). Also respondents were more likely to be active in their communities if their families were not politically active, and to be more supportive of the UK system of government, than those who were more active.

There was a similar positive, if not strong pattern in regard to prior political experiences. For example, a third with such experience felt they could influence change, whilst a quarter of those without prior experience felt they could do this.

DISCUSSION

Despite citizenship being a compulsory part of the school curriculum in England, and despite the focus on creating politically literate and active, responsible citizens, the findings from this survey tend to illustrate a lack of knowledge on the part of many students, and a gulf between attitudes and actions. To an extent, it may be that this reflects the findings of Keating et al. (2010); in their large-scale longitudinal study of citizenship education in England from its inception, they conclude that the young people in the study were more likely to have a positive attitude towards civic and political participation if they had received a lot of specific citizenship teaching, both in terms of curriculum time and specialist teaching. In addition, they noted that there was a cumulative effect, with attitudes strengthening over time based on prior attitudes, that is, positive attitudes aged 16, became more positive for students aged 18. Conversely, those who reported having had little or no citizenship education were significantly more likely to have poor attitudes to participation. Given so many in this study could not remember having been taught citizenship, Keating et al.'s (2010) findings may explain the attitudes reported here and the relatively low levels of participation (although it should be acknowledged that Keating et al.'s study looked at attitudes towards participation and intention to participate rather than actual levels of activity).

On the positive side, the majority of students are generally supportive of democratic structures (if slightly less enthusiastic about the system of government in the UK), are aware of the importance of engaging with civic activities and with the community, and are keen to be informed about the world in which they live. However, it is not clear from where students develop their views. The number of students who claim not to have been taught (a statutory subject) or cannot remember it is relatively high, plus few come from families which are politically active and few have direct personal experience of politics. Most are keen to keep up to date with news, are interested in a range of issues, and so it would seem that many teach themselves what they wish to know, or try to make sense of things as best they can. It would appear from this sample that young people want to know more about civic matters but have not received sufficient education or experience from external support systems. Although it is a positive thing that young people wish to be informed and it would appear to have to do this independently, it is not clear to what extent they are able to examine a range of views and critically engage with issues and so develop well-informed opinions.

Without sufficient knowledge many feel unable to influence matters. Other studies, such as Nelson et al. (2010), have found a connection between high levels of civic knowledge and support for democratic values, and the findings from this survey suggest an association between higher levels of knowledge and positive attitudes and levels of participation. Although students feel participation is important, the majority do not believe they have the ability to influence matters, and consequently, it can be argued they find reasons not to engage in activities. Given a healthy democracy needs active participation by its citizenry, the students' negative perceptions of their ability to influence decisions should be a concern, and reflects findings in other studies (e.g. Keating et al., 2010). Overall, there is a strong sense of disengagement from participants from the civic and political community. The qualitative comments suggest that young people do not feel trusted or respected, whilst in turn their perception of politicians means they do not trust them. Although there is a sense that democracy is a 'good' thing, the level of support for the UK system of government is perceptibly lower.

The lack of political engagement is also seen in the conception of a citizen; most students defined citizenship in terms of community engagement and contributing positively to society, and a good citizen was defined in relation to personal qualities, such as being kind and caring. This stresses what Geboers, Geijsel, Admiraal, and ten Dam (2013) see as a model of 'civil society' where there is an emphasis on social cohesion, coexistence and personal development; this model of citizenship has been criticised by Mead (2010) as a form of communitarianism, which could easily be found in various dictatorships and does little to promote the values of democracy and participation in the political sphere. Although civic engagement is clearly an important element of citizenship, it is a very different conception to models that emphasise a more classical, political model. Part of the problem, as Geboers et al. (2013) imply, is that young people do not yet see themselves as citizens because of the way in which their engagement in the political world is restricted (in the UK, young people are not allowed to vote until the age of 18).

It would seem that citizenship education in England needs a careful reappraisal. Young people generally see the importance of political and civic engagement, yet feel unwilling and/or unable to participate. The resolution to this situation is complex. At one level, it seems there is an argument to develop students' knowledge and understanding of the political, social and community elements of citizenship as envisioned in the original National Curriculum documentation. The range of responses from the students in this survey may reflect the range of approaches different secondary schools are likely to have adopted towards citizenship in the curriculum—schools may teach it as a discrete subject, but others may well have combined it with PSHE, taught it through cross-curricular approaches or specific theme days. It is also highly likely that there are few specialist teachers in these schools. The obvious solution would be to advocate more clearly defined citizenship teaching in the curriculum, taught by specialists. Yet on its own, these are simply 'tinkering' around the edges.

It seems there needs to be a deeper philosophical debate if young people are to value, protect and promote democratic participation in society. The Council of Europe's (2015) educational manifesto questions whether we are doing the right things, in the right way when it comes to education; if, in future, we wish to live in a democratic society, then this must be a fundamental aim of education. As such, citizenship should not simply be a curriculum subject that is 'squeezed' into an overcrowded school time-table; it needs to be one of the driving forces behind curriculum design. It also means that young people should experience democracy in action in schools and the local community; the idea of 'student voice' is not new, but the extent to which young people have a genuine say in their lives, or are given the means and support to allow their voices to be heard, is questionable. At present, the findings from this small survey raise questions about the health of democratic society in England, but the findings resonate with other studies, which in turn suggests the issues raised here need careful and serious attention from all levels of the educational system.

REFERENCES

Benton, T., Cleaver, E., Featherstone, G., Kerr, D., Lopes, J., & Whitby, K. (2008). *Citizenship Education Longitudinal Study (CELS): Sixth annual report young people's civic participation in and beyond school.* London: Department for Children, Schools and Families.

Council of Europe (2015). *Education for change, change for education.* Strasbourg: Council of Europe.

DfE (2011). *The famework for the national curriculum: A report by the expert panel for the national curriculum review.* London: DfE. Retrieved from https://www.gov.uk/government/uploads/system/uploads/attachment_data/file/175439/NCR-Expert_Panel_Report.pdf.

DfE (2013). *National curriculum in England: Citizenship programmes of study for key stages 3 and 4.* London: DfE. Retrieved from https://www.gov.uk/government/publications/national-curriculum-in-england-citizenship-programmes-of-study/national-curriculum-in-england-citizenship-programmes-of-study-for-key-stages-3-and-4.

DfEE/QCA (1999). *Citizenship: The national curriculum for England.* London: DfEE/QCA.

Dinesen, P. T., Nørgaard, A. S., & Klemmensen, R. (2014). The civic personality: Personality and democratic citizenship. *Political Studies, 62,* 134–152. doi:10.1111/1467-9248.12094.

Faulks, K. (2006). Education for citizenship in England's secondary schools: A critique of current principle and practice. *Journal of Education Policy, 21*(1), 59–74. doi:10.1080/02680930500391546.

Geboers, E., Geijsel, F., Admiraal, W., & ten Dam, G. (2013). Review of the effects of citizenship education. *Educational Research Review, 9,* 158–173.

Harris, R. (2006). Editorial: A special issue on citizenship education. *Prospero, 12*(3), 3–5.

Home Office (2004). *2003 Home Office Citizenship Survey: People, families and communities.* London: Home Office.

Ireland, E., Kerr, D., Lopes, J., Nelson, J., & Cleaver, E. (2006). *Active citizenship and young people: Opportunities, experiences and challenges in and beyond school citizenship education longitudinal study: Fourth annual report.* Nottingham: Department for Education and Skills.

Isac, M. M., Maslowski, R., Creemers, B., & van der Werf, W. (2014). The contribution of schooling to secondary school students' citizenship outcomes across countries. *School Effectiveness and School Improvement, 25*(1), 29–63.

Keating, A., Kerr, D., Benton, T., Mundy, E., & Lopes, J. (2010). *Citizenship education in England 2001–2010: Young people's practices and prospects for the future: The eighth and final report from the Citizenship Education Longitudinal Study (CELS).* London: Department for Education.

Keating, A., Kerr, D., Lopes, J., Featherstone, G., & Benton, T. (2009). *Embedding citizenship education in secondary schools in England (2002–08): Citizenship education longitudinal study seventh annual report*. London: Department for Children, Schools and Families.

Kerr, D. (2005). England's teenagers fail the patriotic test: The lessons from England's participation in the IEA Civic Education Survey. In S. Wilde (Ed.), *Political and citizenship education* (pp. 29–47). Didcot: Symposium Books.

Kerr, D., Cleaver, E., Ireland, E., & Blenkinsop, S. (2003). *Citizenship Education Longitudinal Study first crosssectional survey 2001–2002*. Nottingham: DfES.

Kerr, D., Lopes, J., Nelson, J., White, K., Cleaver, E., & Benton, T. (2007). *Vision versus pragmatism: Citizenship in the secondary school curriculum in England citizenship education longitudinal study: Fifth annual report*. London: Department for Education and Skills.

Kiwan, D. (2008). Citizenship education in England at the cross-roads? Four models of citizenship and their implications for ethnic and religious diversity. *Oxford Review of Education, 34*(1), 39–58. doi:10.1080/03054980701584551.

Lopes, J., Benton, T., & Cleaver, E. (2009). Young people's intended civic and political participation: Does education matter? *Journal of Youth Studies, 12*(1), 1–20. doi:10.1080/13676260802191920.

Mead, N. (2010). Conflicting conceptions of participation in secondary school citizenship. *Pastoral Care in Education, 28*(1), 45–57.

Metzger, A., & Smetana, J. G. (2010). Social cognitive development and adolescent civic engagement. In L. R. Sherrod, J. Torney-Purtha, & C. A. Flanagan (Eds.), *Handbook of research on civic engagement in youth* (pp. 221–248). Hoboken, NJ: John Wiley & Sons, Inc.

Nelson, J., Wade, P., & Kerr, D. (2010). *Young people's civic attitudes and practies: England's outcomes from the IEA International Civic and Citizenship Education Study*. Slough: NFER.

Ofsted (2004). *Ofsted subject reports 2002/03: Citizenship in secondary schools*. London: Ofsted.

Ofsted (2005). *Citizenship in secondary schools: Evidence from Ofsted inspections (2003/04)*. London: Ofsted.

Ofsted (2010). *Citizenship established? Citizenship in schools 2006/09*. London: Ofsted.

Ofsted (2013). *Citizenship consolidated? A survey of citizenship in schools between 2009 and 2012*. London: Ofsted.

Pring, R. (2006). Against citizenship. *Prospero, 12*(3), 54–58.

QCA (1998). *Education for citizenship and the teaching of democracy in schools*. London: QCA.

QCA (2007). *Citizenship: Programme of study for key stage 3 and attainment target*. London: QCA.

UK Political Info (n.d.). *General election turnout 1945–2015*. Retrieved from http://www.ukpolitical.info/Turnout10.htm.

CHAPTER 4

Youth Civic Engagement in Hong Kong: A Glimpse into Two Systems Under One China

Liz Jackson, Puja Kapai, Shiru Wang, and Ching Yin Leung

This chapter examines youth perceptions regarding civic engagement during a tumultuous time in Hong Kong.[1] We begin by examining the historical context of Hong Kong, tracing changes in its political status and educational system in relation to the civic attitudes and behaviors of its population over time, particularly as Hong Kong shifted from a colony of the British Empire to a Special Administrative Region (SAR) of the People's Republic of China toward the end of the twentieth century. Next, the chapter discusses the findings of a study of Hong Kong youth perceptions of civic engagement, comparing the views of youth with two distinct prior experiences of civic education: university students in Hong Kong who were previously educated in Hong Kong or Mainland China. The study reveals significant differences between these groups, with important implications for reforming civic education in Hong Kong.

L. Jackson (✉) • P. Kapai • S. Wang • C.Y. Leung
Division of Policy, Administration and Social Sciences Education,
University of Hong Kong, Pok Fu Lam, Hong Kong
e-mail: lizjackson@hku.hk

© The Author(s) 2017   59
C. Broom (ed.), *Youth Civic Engagement in a Globalized World*,
Palgrave Studies in Global Citizenship Education and Democracy,
DOI 10.1057/978-1-137-56533-4_4

UNDERSTANDING CITIZEN IDENTITY IN HONG KONG

Political identity and citizenship education are at major crossroads today in Hong Kong. Hong Kong has a complex and unique political history and status. It has never been a nation or state, and its political status and government have transformed dramatically, with little direct input from its population. For most of the twentieth century, it was a colony of the British Empire. It was populated by Chinese immigrants and a small percentage of ethnic minorities, who joined Hong Kong's indigenous populations and ethnic minority soldiers stationed there as part of the British Armed Forces in the 1840s. From the 1980s to the Handover, a major transformation of Hong Kong's political culture took place, involving the introduction of political parties, the establishment of the Ombudsman, and the enactment of a range of laws for implementing Hong Kong's human rights obligations under international treaties (including the Bill of Rights Ordinance, the Sex Discrimination Ordinance, the Family Status Discrimination Ordinance, and the Disability Discrimination Ordinance). In 1995, a fully democratic Legislative Council (LegCo) was elected for the first time.

In 1997, in accordance with the Peking Convention of 1898 and reaffirmed under the 1984 Sino-British Joint Declaration, Hong Kong was "handed over" to China under a "One country, two systems" framework, recognizing and preserving the inherent social, economic, legal, and political differences while binding the systems of Hong Kong and China together for a period of 50 years. Under the British, Hong Kong was ruled in a liberal manner, in line with the British common law tradition and a free market economy. The Basic Law of Hong Kong (Basic Law) entrenches continuity of laws and systems previously in force (including civil and political rights guaranteed under the law), allowing Hong Kong to exercise a high degree of autonomy as an SAR, barring matters pertaining to foreign affairs and defense. In contrast, China is a one-party authoritarian society, with limited civil and political rights. While China was during most of the twentieth century inward facing, isolationist, and nationalistic, Hong Kong has always been more outward facing, global, and liberal in political culture (Lee, 2008).

On the other hand, the Hong Kong government is institutionally subordinate to the Beijing government, with the city's Chief Executive elected by and accountable to a tightly controlled Electoral College. The Standing Committee of the National People's Congress of China (NPCSC) has power of final interpretation of the city's mini-constitution. The Hong Kong government has been and continues to be one of limited representativeness, given the predominance of sector-based functional constituencies in the election of the Chief Executive of Hong Kong and half of the LegCo. The voting procedures enable government-initiated proposals to be passed by simple majority, whereas private members' bills and proposals require a majority in each constituency. This has enabled government and business interests to collude to ignore the interests of working classes and marginalized groups (Kapai, 2011).

The LegCo is increasingly mired in stalemates due to filibustering, tactical challenges, and quorum calls to frustrate the opposition at every opportunity. Although Hong Kong has a number of political parties, there is no political party law to regulate them. The stronghold of functional constituencies and the predominance of pro-Beijing parties have further intensified conflict as common people struggle to influence policies and laws (Kapai, 2011). A decade after being promised, universal suffrage remains elusive. Pan-democrats have made numerous attempts (including holding a de facto referendum by triggering by-elections by resigning from their seats in LegCo) to push for further democratization in Hong Kong. As 2017 drew closer, it was anticipated that the NPCSC would set out a framework to ensure a smooth transitioning to a more democratic system for the legislature to enact the necessary laws by 2015 for implementation in the 2016 LegCo elections.

To put pressure on Beijing, in 2013, the idea of "Occupy Central with Love and Peace" (OCLP) was floated by Benny Tai, an associate professor of law (later joined by another professor and a Baptist minister), recommending that if the proposed framework failed to meet international standards of universal suffrage, Hong Kong people would stage a peaceful, civil disobedience movement. To address concerns that it would be disruptive and cause losses to the economy and to minimize opposition from the working class, a public holiday on 1 October was designated as the date of the sit-in in the Central business district.

On August 31, 2014, the NPCSC set out a framework for the implementation of universal suffrage for the election of the members of the LegCo in 2016 and the Chief Executive in 2017. However, the methods for determining eligibility to stand as a candidate for Chief Executive imposed significant constraints, effectively screening out candidates from opposing political camps. It was also stipulated that if the package did not pass, the election of the next LegCo by universal suffrage would be postponed to 2021. The filtering of candidates based on their political orientation under the proposed framework was an affront to international standards of democracy, universal suffrage, and free and fair elections and a violation of the guarantees under the Basic Law, leading Hong Kong people to the streets in protest.

Student organizations occupied the Forecourt 2014 at Civic Square outside the Government Headquarters in Admiralty on 26 September, and surrounding areas in subsequent days, paralyzing entry and exit routes as they amassed steadily growing crowds in support, numbering 100,000 at the height of the movement, which lasted 79 days. On 28 September, OCLP leaders proclaimed the student movement as the beginning of OCLP. Student leaders played a pioneering role in turning the protest sites into laboratories of civic participation by organizing class boycotts, street assemblies with educational lectures, study stations, food and first-aid stations, as well as a counseling group to address intergenerational conflict over the movement's means and ends. The student leaders and OCLP protesters attracted swathes of supporters after the police's use of tear gas to disperse unarmed and peaceful crowds, who used umbrellas in defense against pepper spray and tear gas, earning the movement the title of the "Umbrella Movement," with the yellow umbrella as its signature symbol.

The scale of the movement and its organization and activities broke new ground in the history of movement building in Hong Kong, coopting public sites as spaces for civic participation and solidarity by design and action, yielding a profound impact on political consciousness and civil society (Lam, 2015). It became a hub for civic engagement in the most politically significant locales and the liveliest districts of Mong Kok, Causeway Bay, and Tsim Sha Tsui. Each of the Occupy sites had communities engaged in civic activity with participants of various backgrounds, including district and legislative counselors, former civil servants, professors, students, and members of the legal profession, and ordinary Hong Kong folk, including ethnic minorities as well as tourists, discussing Hong Kong's future.

In the last 18 years, Hong Kong's people have experienced numerous challenges that have tested their faith in capitalism and the Hong Kong government's ability and willingness to help common people instead of pandering to corporate elites who can reward leaders with their votes. Widening income disparities, stagnant wages with rising inflation, a greater number of households falling below the poverty line, the lack of affordable housing and continued prevalence of caged homes, lack of an adequate retirement plan for the city's aging population, and increased competition for city resources due to steady growth in Mainland families are some of the issues dominating the lives of Hong Kong people. The youth experience tremendous pressure under Hong Kong's exam-oriented education system and increasingly feel pessimistic about their prospects in light of Hong Kong's systemic failures in addressing these issues.

Though the vast majority of Hong Kong's population (some 90 %) is ethnically Han Chinese (the majority in Mainland), after the Cultural Revolution, those in Hong Kong have increasingly seen themselves as distinct from their Mainland counterparts. Under the one-way permit scheme, Mainland Chinese residents are eligible to apply for residence in Hong Kong (Article 22(4), Basic Law) with the aim of facilitating the reunification of cross-border families. To date, the scheme has facilitated the entry of nearly one million Mainland Chinese into Hong Kong. Hong Kong people view new immigrants from the Mainland as competitors for limited resources and opportunities. After the Court of Final Appeal's ruling that Chinese children born in Hong Kong would automatically acquire the right of abode (*Director of Immigration v. Chong Fung Yuen*, 2 HKLRD 533), Mainland Chinese mothers began to come to Hong Kong to give birth to take advantage of its favorable position, resulting in a critical shortage of hospital beds for Hong Kong mothers. In the 10 years since the decision, 170,000 children born to Mainland Chinese parents obtained permanent residence in Hong Kong, competing with children of Hong Kong resident parents for educational and medical resources. Moreover, Mainland tourists and smugglers come into Hong Kong to sweep up necessities for parallel trading in China, as goods are either more expensive or scarce there, such as baby formula and diapers of particular brands.

Such tensions have persisted and escalated, culminating in the organization of groups such as Hong Kong Indigenous and other "localists" who emphasize Hong Kong identity, sometimes described in opposition to or as anti-Mainland Chinese, and even labeling Mainland immigrants in Hong Kong as "locusts" in 2012. These sentiments are fueled by a lack of trust in the Chinese government. When asked about their identity, in the 1990s and beyond, fluctuations and ambivalence have marked responses to polls, with some members of the population identifying as "Hong Kong people," while others would categorize themselves as "Chinese Hongkongers" or "Hong Kong Chinese" (Chung, 2016).

CIVIC EDUCATION AND ATTITUDES IN HONG KONG
AND CHINA

Civic education developed along different paths in Hong Kong and China. In the latter, national education has been a central feature of education since the Cultural Revolution. Today, patriotic education continues to systematically impact Mainland Chinese youth, through formal educational policy and curriculum, as well as public, media, family, and cultural campaigns (Fairbrother, 2003). Its goals include inculcating loyalty and a sense of affection and superiority regarding the country, its government, and economic orientation. Thus, civic education has been substantiated through textbooks, curriculum guidelines, assessment procedures, and informal, public channels. Throughout the 1990s and 2000s, Mainland Chinese youth identified secondary education as having the biggest impact on their political views (Fairbrother, 2003).

In Hong Kong, civic education has been largely absent when compared with other societies (Jackson, 2014). Historically, the British took a laissez-faire approach to schooling during much of the twentieth century, and assimilationism toward a culture or political entity was not a major goal of the educational system (Sweeting, 1992). During and after the Cultural Revolution, the British mandated *apolitical* total school environments (from the classroom to extracurricular activities) in government schools (Fairbrother, 2003; Jackson, 2014; Vickers, 2005). Youth and educators were forbidden from expressing any political messages, for or against the British Empire or China. In anticipation of the Handover, civic education emerged on the policy agenda; schools and teachers were encouraged to incorporate elements into the curriculum to prepare students through understanding and appreciation. However, such recommendations carried less weight than other reforms during that time (Fairbrother, 2003; Jackson, 2014; Leung & Ng, 2004).

Since the 1980s, civic education in Hong Kong ("Civic and Moral Education") has inched forward at the policy level, with guidelines calling for enhancing socialization and positively orienting students toward "One country, two systems" (Fairbrother, 2003; Jackson, 2014). Yet at the same time, public ambivalence toward unification increased. Teachers who have been active in civic education in the twenty-first century have typically focused on the cultural and traditional commonalities of Hong Kong and China, avoiding political aspects (Lai & Byram, 2012). Fairbrother (2003) found that Mainland Chinese youth were far more patriotic than Hong

Kong youth, who were ambivalent, if not negative, about modern China and its politics and symbols. They noted that they share some common beliefs, practices, and traditions, but had few positive views about national politics and government.

In part as a response to the growing rift between the societies and Hong Kong's anti-Mainland stance and growing identity crisis, particularly among Hong Kong's youth, in 2011, the Education Bureau devised guidelines for moral and national education as a new subject in school timetables. The curriculum contained learning outcomes related to increasing affection toward Mainland China, appreciation for its form of government, and related positive feelings (CDC, 2012). Model syllabi were provided, and funding was allocated to private organizations for developing resources, including a now-infamous *China Model* text, which compared Mainland Chinese policies favorably to those of western societies and obscured problems in China historically or today (CDC, 2012; Chou, 2012; Jackson, 2014).

The result was a mass public outcry against patriotic/nationalistic curriculum. In the summer of 2012, educators, youth, and parents organized wide scale protests against the implementation of this curriculum, which many equated with brainwashing, wary in relation to their perceptions of civic education's impact in Mainland China (Chou, 2012; Jackson, 2014). Critics charged that this curriculum overlapped with other recent reforms, notably "Liberal Studies," introduced in 2009, which also discusses Mainland China (Jackson, 2014). The government has since shelved the proposal for national education indefinitely. But of particular significance to note here is the organization and leadership of the protests by youths aged 14–15, who staged a sit-in outside the Government Headquarters demanding the government withdraw the proposal. This was Hong Kong's first coordinated youth movement since the protests in 1984. Joshua Wong and his group Scholarism sowed the seeds for youth activism that year. This movement sparked a change in the landscape of civic participation and played a foundational role in the 2014 Umbrella Movement.

Today, civic education in Hong Kong schools continues as piecemeal learning about relevant legal frameworks and how to contribute to Hong Kong, China, and/or the world. Liberal Studies introduces information about China, as well as the significance of capitalism (Jackson, 2015), in a curriculum focused in part on problem-solving skills. As the society and its youth population become increasingly political outside of schools, schoolteachers are endeavoring to provide a politically neutral education to students (EPU, 2015), lest they be accused of playing a role in unrest. In this tumultuous time, we sought to gauge young adults' views about their experiences in relation to the meaning and nature of civic engagement within Hong Kong.

OUR STUDY

Our team employed a survey developed based upon the conceptual model and questionnaire discussed in Chap. 1. Our survey was open to undergraduate students at the University of Hong Kong, Hong Kong's oldest and most international public tertiary institution. Participants were recruited from eight large (i.e., more than 100 students per class) undergraduate classes with diverse student intakes by nationality and major. The classes primarily served first- and second-year students and were interdisciplinary general studies courses required for graduation. The survey was open to all students in these classes across majors, nationalities, year of university study, and age, with some 17-year-olds participating, in line with enrolment norms and research ethics practices of the university. Though 17 may seem young according to international norms, as the most frequent protesters in Hong Kong in recent years have come from secondary schools (more so than universities), our team could identify no rationale for excluding younger university students from participation. Surveys were administered via Google Surveys online and were open from mid-October to mid-November 2015.

Given Hong Kong's legal and political context, it was essential to include separate questions related to Hong Kong and China's government systems, and use locally relevant measures of student background, socioeconomic status, and so on. Additionally, we sought to capture opinions and views based on local-level affiliation and engagement, national-level affiliation and engagement with China, and potential global connections. We were interested in understanding participants' level of civic engagement in relation to their political views, those of their family, and their recollections of their civic, citizenship, and/or government/political education. Anticipating dissimilarities based on differences in Hong Kong and China, we sought to compare participants' views based on the society they were educated in (Hong Kong or Mainland China). In this chapter, we focus on students from Hong Kong and China (excluding international student data). Data were entered into SPSS and analyzed using descriptive statistics and cross-tabs. Quotations have been copy edited to correct basic grammar and punctuation errors.

LIMITATIONS

The survey administration period coincided with a tumultuous time in the participating university's internal politics, which may have impacted students in relation to their civic participation. Concerns with academic freedom at the university were on the rise during the study period in relation to the delayed and then rejected appointment of law professor (and former dean) Johannes Chan in 2015 to the post of pro-vice-chancellor of academic affairs and resources. As Chan was publicly supportive toward his colleague Benny Tai, leading initiator of OCPL (associated with but also distinct from the primarily youth-driven Umbrella Movement), while the University Council is made up of many pro-government appointees including direct appointments by the Hong Kong Chief Executive, the rejection of Chan's appointment provoked an outcry due to the decision's suspected political motivations, which overrode an international search committee's unanimous recommendation for his appointment to the post. Despite leaks of the Council members' views and concern over the lack of reasonable basis for the rejection, due to confidentiality rules and the Council's lack of transparency, no official explanation has been proffered for the rejection. University students have organized alongside faculty organizations to protest this decision and call for restructuring and/or independent reviews, a stronger stance toward academic freedom of faculty, and related initiatives.

Our survey may not be perfectly representative of student views, owing to the voluntary nature of respondent participation. In each class in which participants were recruited, it was emphasized that student views across the political spectrum (and beyond it) were of value, and that students should participate for research purposes regardless of their political views at the university, local community, national, and/or international levels. Finally, the university population is not necessarily representative of the larger youth population, as it includes proportionately more students from middle class and working class backgrounds (rather than those living in poverty). Students from Mainland China generally represent the upper part of the spectrum of Chinese youth in terms of political connections and socioeconomic class. Nonetheless, our findings reflect a great diversity of political views, within Hong Kong and across Hong Kong and Mainland China, and social class diversity as well, as summarized in the next section. Moreover, despite the politicized climate in relation to university politics, given the increase in perceived interference with university affairs across Hong Kong by the Chief Executive (de facto head of all public universities in Hong Kong), the survey's potential to capture the relationship between past and present activism, personal and family experiences, and opinions in relation to politics and broader socioeconomic and livelihood issues in Hong Kong is not only timely but unique and unprecedented at this historic juncture and will advance knowledge of youth civic engagement in Hong Kong as the SAR edges closer toward the expiry of its 50-year "grace period" of maintaining its present political, legal, and economic system.

FINDINGS: HONG KONG AND MAINLAND CHINESE YOUTH

Findings are summarized in Table 4.1.

Three hundred and sixty-six local students (students who grew up in Hong Kong) participated (approximately 3 % of the local undergraduate university population), including 180 males and 185 females. Over half (57 %) lived in privately owned property, while most others lived in public housing (18 %), government/company housing (12 %), or rented housing (11 %). (This compares to 54 % in private housing, and 46 % in public housing across Hong Kong; HKHA, 2015.) More than half (54 %) were Year 1 students. About one-third (33 %) were in Year 2, and the rest in Years 3 and 4 (13 % each). Roughly representative of overall enrolments, most were enrolled in Faculties of Arts, Business and Economics, Engineering, Medicine, and Science (14–17 % each), with less in Architecture, Dentistry, Education, Law, and Social Sciences (5–10 % each). Most (84 %) were 18–20 years old. The majority (95 %) had lived in Hong Kong more than 10 years and received their secondary education there.

Thirty-six students from Mainland China participated (approximately 2 % of Mainland students at the university). This group consisted of 16 males and 20 females. Two-thirds were living in rented housing, or in university halls, while others lived in private property or government/company housing. Most were in Years 1 and 2 (40 % each), with smaller groups in Years 3 (6 %) and 4 (14 %). Most were enrolled in the Faculty of Business and Economics (39 %), Science (31 %), and Engineering (19 %). Most (72 %) were 18–20 years old. More than half (58 %) had lived in Hong Kong between 1 and 3 years with others living in Hong Kong less than one year (36 %). Most (95 %) received their secondary education in China.

Table 4.1 Hong Kong summary of findings

Hong Kong youth	Number of participants: 336 Hong Kong (HK) students & 36 Mainland students			
Demographics				
Gender	Male: 180 (49.2 %) 16 (44.4 %)	Female: 185 (50.5 %) 20 (55.6 %)	Other/ Undisclosed: 1 (0.3 %) 0 (0 %)	
Cultural Identification	Hong Kong: 110 (30 %) 1 (2.8 %)	Chinese: 207 (56.6 %) 33 (91.6 %)	Other: 24 (6.6 %) 1 (2.8 %)	Undisclosed: 25 (6.8 %) 1 (2.8 %)
First Language	Cantonese: 276 (75.4 %) 1 (2.8 %)	Chinese/Mandarin: 49 (13.4 %) 34 (94.4 %)	Other: 15 (4.1 %) 0 (0 %)	Undisclosed: 26 (7.1 %) 1 (2.8 %)
Citizenship education	Yes 199 (54.4 %) 14 (38.9 %)	No 100 (27.3 %) 18 (50 %)	Do not remember 67 (18.3 %) 4 (11.1 %)	
Political knowledge	Very knowledgeable 20 (5.5 %) 2 (5.6 %)	Some knowledge 224 (61.2 %) 19 (52.8 %)	Little knowledge 122 (33.3 %) 15 (41.7 %)	
Follow the news	Always 81 (22.1 %) 9 (25 %)	Occasionally 219 (59.8 %) 20 (55.6 %)	Rarely 62 (16.9 %) 6 (16.7 %)	Not at all 4 (1.1 %) 1 (2.8 %)
Personal political/ public affairs experience	Yes 193 (52.7 %) 11 (30.6 %)	No 138 (37.7 %) 25 (69.4 %)	Do not remember 35 (9.6 %) 0 (0 %)	Undisclosed 0 (0 %) 0 (0 %)
Family's political involvement	62 (16.9 %) 3 (8.3 %)	262 (71.6 %) 30 (83.3 %)	27 (7.4 %) 0 (0 %)	15 (4.1 %) 3 (8.3 %)
Personality type	Assertive	Amiable	Humanistic	Analytical

(*continued*)

Table 4.1   (continued)

Hong Kong youth — Number of participants: 336 Hong Kong (HK) students & 36 Mainland students

(In each cell: HK figure, with the *Mainland figure in italics* below.)

Attitude to community engagement

Very important	Neutral	Somewhat important	Not important
48 (13.1 %)	90 (24.6 %)	105 (28.7 %)	123 (33.6 %)
3 (8.3 %)	*12 (33.3 %)*	*4 (11.1 %)*	*17 (47.2 %)*

Attitude to participation of civic processes

Very important	Somewhat important	Not important
178 (48.6 %)	183 (50 %)	5 (1.4 %)
13 (36.1 %)	*23 (63.9 %)*	*0 (0%)*

Important	Neutral	Not important	Does not matter
198 (54.1 %)	157 (42.9 %)	4 (1.1 %)	7 (1.9 %)
6 (16.7 %)	*28 (77.8 %)*	*1 (2.8%)*	*1 (2.8%)*

1 = Limited autonomy (emphasis upon China's sovereignty over Hong Kong) vs. 7 = Pro-autonomy (emphasis upon Hong Kong's autonomy)

	1	2	3	4	5	6	7	Does not matter
Personal political views (a) Undisclosed: 13 (3.6 %) *Undisclosed: 2 (5.6%)*	2 (0.5 %) *9 (2.5%)*	8 (2.2 %) *4 (11.1%)*	12 (3.3 %) *6 (16.7%)*	56 (15.3 %) *11 (30.6%)*	72 (19.7 %) *3 (8.3%)*	118 (32.2 %) *1 (2.8%)*	85 (23.2 %) *0 (0%)*	
Parents' political views (a) Undisclosed: 15 (4.1 %) *Undisclosed: 3 (8.3%)*	15 (4.1 %) *8 (22.2%)*	61 (16.7 %) *7 (19.4%)*	61 (16.7 %) *6 (16.7%)*	106 (29 %) *10 (27.8%)*	54 (14.8) *1 (2.8%)*	43 (11.7 %) *1 (2.8%)*	11 (3.0 %) *0 (0%)*	

1 = Conservative vs. 7 = Liberal

Hong Kong youth	*Number of participants: 336 Hong Kong (HK) students & 36 Mainland students*						
	Very supportive	Supportive	Neutral	Not supportive	Against it		Do not care
Personal political views (b) Undisclosed: 13 (3.6%) *Undisclosed: 2 (5.6%)*	0 (0%) *3 (8.3%)*	6 (1.6%) *1 (2.8%)*	16 (4.4%) *4 (11.1%)*	49 (13.4%) *18 (50%)*	72 (19.7%) *3 (8.3%)*	121 (33.1%) *4 (11.1%)*	89 (24.3%) *1 (2.8%)*
Parents' political views (b) Undisclosed: 16 (4.4%) *Undisclosed: 3 (8.3%)*	18 (4.9%) *6 (16.7%)*	69 (18.9%) *7 (19.4%)*	74 (20.2%) *6 (16.7%)*	90 (24.6%) *12 (33.3%)*	48 (13.1%) *1 (2.8%)*	39 (10.7%) *1 (2.8%)*	12 (3.3%) *0 (0%)*
Level of personal efficacy	**Effective** 30 (8.2%) *5 (13.9%)*		**A little effective** 282 (77%) *27 (75%)*		**Not effective** 54 (14.8%) *4 (11.1%)*		
Civic involvement Undisclosed: 80 (21.9%) *Undisclosed: 8 (22.2%)*	**Active** 15 (4.1%) *0 (0%)*		**Occasionally active** 155 (42.3%) *14 (38.9%)*		**Not active** 116 (31.7%) *14 (38.9%)*		

(continued)

Table 4.1   (continued)

Hong Kong youth	Number of participants: 336 Hong Kong (HK) students & 36 Mainland students					
Attitudes toward democracy (Undisclosed: 50 (13.7%)) (*Undisclosed: 6 (16.7%)*)	50 (13.75) *4 (11.1%)*	192 (52.5%) *12 (33.3%)*	66 (18%) *12 (33.3%)*	1 (0.3%) *1 (2.8%)*	2 (0.5%) *0 (0%)*	5 (1.4%) *1 (2.8%)*
Attitude toward govt. system in China (Undisclosed: 51 (13.9%)) (*Undisclosed: 6 (16.7%)*)	1 (0.3%) *2 (5.6%)*	8 (2.2%) *10 (27.8%)*	68 (18.65) *12 (33.3%)*	111 (30.3%) *5 (13.9%)*	114 (31.1%) *0 (0%)*	13 (3.6%) *1 (2.8%)*
Attitude toward govt. system in Hong Kong (Undisclosed: 39 (10.7%)) (*Undisclosed: 4 (11.1%)*)	8 (2.2%) *0 (0%)*	60 (16.45) *2 (5.6%)*	161 (44%) *19 (52.8%)*	66 (18%) *1 (2.8%)*	16 (4.4%) *0 (0%)*	16 (4.4%) *10 (27.8%)*

Students' civic participation (HK students) (Top 3)	Often	Seldom	Sometimes	Never	Mean	SD
Being a good neighbor	26 7.1%	124 33.9%	154 42.1%	62 16.9%	1.69	0.84
Following political news	42 11.5%	103 28.1%	151 41.3%	70 19.1%	1.68	0.91

Hong Kong youth	Number of participants: 336 Hong Kong (HK) students & 36 Mainland students					
	Often	Seldom	Sometimes	Never	Mean	SD
Helping those in need	20	145	165	36	1.59	0.74
	5.5 %	39.6 %	45.1 %	9.8 %		
Students' civic participation (mainland students) (Top 3)	*Often*	*Seldom*	*Sometimes*	*Never*	*Mean*	*SD*
Being a good neighbor	*1*	*6*	*14*	*15*	*2.19*	*0.82*
	2.8%	*16.7%*	*38.9%*	*41.7%*		
Helping those in need	*2*	*11*	*19*	*4*	*1.69*	*0.75*
	5.6%	*30.6%*	*52.8%*	*11.1%*		
Following political news	*7*	*11*	*7*	*11*	*1.61*	*1.13*
	19.4%	*30.6%*	*19.4%*	*30.6%*		

Figure in **bold italics** indicated data from 36 students from Mainland China

About half (54 %) of local respondents and just over one-third of (39 %) Mainland respondents indicated they learned civic education, civics, and/or government content in secondary school. Local respondents noted learning about the political and legal system/legislation (40 %) as well as issues relating to voting/election (38 %), government structure and operation (32 %), and separation of powers (27 %). Civil disobedience (19 %) as well as civil rights and responsibilities and civic education (16 %) were also mentioned. With less student data available for the Mainland Chinese group, broadly, respondents recalled learning about government structure and selection, as well as voting age.

Most (80 %) local respondents expressed that such education was useful or quite useful. Such respondents added that their learning had increased their awareness of social and political issues and problems and helped them better understand their rights and responsibilities and to be more aware of what is happening in society and the government. Some also felt that what they learned stimulated critical thinking and reflection. Those who felt what they learned was not useful expressed they had not been able to relate what they learned to daily life. While the structures of government seemed complicated to some, others were not interested in the topics or learned only at the surface level.

A different picture emerged among Mainland Chinese respondents. Most articulated that what they learned was not useful, as they did not feel they could enjoy civil rights as described in textbooks. Though they have the right to vote at 18, they understood that their right is qualified by being "under the supervision of government" (student #153), and is actually "quite limited" (student #451). One respondent expressed complex views:

> What I remember most about is the government structure and how so called democratic socialism with Chinese characteristic works in China. My feeling is complex. First, due to the undeveloped condition in China, I understand we have to walk our special way out, because the western approach may not be applicable for the old China, and surely I love my motherland though it has a lot of problems; on the other hand, it is kind of ridiculous to frequently hear the government vaunt itself for being efficient and democratic. Surely, we know bureaucracy and corruption are still there. (student #211)

Most (60 %) local and Mainland respondents claimed to follow news occasionally. The vast majority of local respondents (93 %) followed local news, with most (62 %) also following global and some also following national (Chinese) news (42 %). Among Mainland respondents, most (86 %) followed global news and national news (75 %), while 25 % followed local (Hong Kong) news. Reasons local respondents gave for following local news included that it was more relevant to their lives, and more readily accessible. However, many also followed global news to gain a global perspective and stay connected to the rest of the world:

> As a local Hongkonger, I should and wish to know more about what is happening around our city. And as Hong Kong is an international city, I hope to develop a global perspective to view things and understand how international issues will affect our city. (student #167)

Local respondents who followed national news cited interest in Mainland China and its relevance to their studies, lives, and/or future. Similarly, Mainland Chinese respondents indicated following local news due to being interested in what is happening around them, and followed global news to track issues around the world:

> I was born in Mainland China so I am interested in things happening there. Local events happen around us and may affect our live. Also international events can have significant impact on China and Hong Kong. (student #26)

> I am concerned with the situation in my homeland and also have a lot of interest in global issues. (student #484)

Half (53 %) of local respondents participated in public affairs in the past two years, and most (74 %) of these respondents indicated their participation affected their views on politics and government. The impact was largely related to their experience in the Umbrella Movement. Many felt more dissatisfied with the government than before. For instance, a respondent commented:

> I joined the Umbrella Movement last year, and I lived there for 2 months, working for a voluntary first-aid station. There I talked to people from all walks of life, including district counselors, former civil servants, journalists, tourists, and students. It was surprising to me as I found that people can look at one thing with totally different perspectives...Also, it made me feel desperate towards the current government regime, which can hear the people's voice, but pretends not to listen. I have been asking myself how an ideal society or government should be since the movement. (student #97)

Some local students involved in charity work felt the government should do more for the public:

> The experience did affect my view on government. When I was doing home visits to people living in subdivided flats, I was shocked by how the Hong Kong government treats them. Although the rent for subdivided flat is very high, the government does not provide any subsidy or flat...[people] used more than half of their income to pay the rent. This leaves me with a bad impression of the government. (student #384)

Those who reported their experience had no impact on their views toward the government were mainly involved in community and charity work unassociated with political parties or issues; a few also added that they had a pessimistic view beforehand:

> No, I already realized that the government rarely listens to the public's opinions. (student #12)

> No, I always think that the government is unfair. (student #345)

> No, because our government rarely listens to our voice. (student #421)

Nearly one-third (31 %) of Mainland respondents participated in public affairs in the past two years, but only four indicated their participation affected their views on politics or government. Others who engaged in civil affairs reported that the events they joined were not related to politics, so their participation had not affected their views.

In contrast with the local respondents themselves, few (17 %) reported that their families were active in political activities. Of this group, nearly half (45 %) reported that their parents were against the government or not satisfied with the government and would express their views through voting, protest, demonstrations, or discussions. Respondents whose parents reportedly supported the government (27 %) likewise expressed this by voting or discussions. Among Mainland respondents, three (8 %) reported that their families were active in political activities. Their comments reflect their parents complaining or reacting to government decisions and policies:

> My parents are CCP members, who support the decisions from the CCP. However, they do complain of political affairs... (student #153)

> They feel powerless to change anything. But they like to predict what the government is going to do and act accordingly. Especially, [in relation] to economy. (student #29)

Almost all (99 %) of local and Mainland respondents expressed it was important or somewhat important for people to be actively involved in improving their communities:

> As everyone is part of the society, it is one's responsibility to be involved in the community and help in improving it. (student #234)

> I believe it's the collective efforts of every citizen to bring Hong Kong towards a better future, therefore it's important for people to be actively involved in improving their communities. (student #201)

Yet the majority of local respondents (77 %) felt their actions had only a little impact to change society, while twice as many felt their actions were not at all effective (15 %) in contrast with those who regarded their actions as effective (8 %). Similarly, Mainland respondents felt individual efforts had limited influence on society. Many local respondents expressed having lost confidence in the government based on the government responses to recent political events. Others expressed that they did not feel their actions were effective as the governments of Hong Kong and China were not listening to the voices of the people:

> Honestly, people like me have very little power in society. No matter what you do, especially if you're in China, it's never up to you—it'll always be up to the government. To say otherwise would be lying to oneself. It's unrealistic to think that the actions of a person [like] me can really bring change. The most it can do is to motivate change, to inspire others who hold a higher status to see the reality of an issue... (student #157)

> From national education to the umbrella revolution, we can see that the government won't listen to the opposing voice echoing in the society... (student #375)

Among local and Mainland respondents, the three civic processes they engaged most often in were being a good neighbor, following political news, and helping those in need. The three least popular activities among local respondents were joining civic groups, citizen journalism, and joining a political party. For Mainland respondents, the three least engaged processes were writing to government officials or newspapers, protesting, and boycotting. Among local respondents who participated in civic activity, most began their civic activities between the ages of 16 and 19 (39 %) or 13 and 15 (20 %). The majority of these respondents had joined the Umbrella Movement and/or did volunteering work, such as fundraising for non-governmental organisations (NGOs) or visiting the elderly, joining demonstrations or protests, or participating in university related activities (15 %). Sixteen percent of students were six- to nine-year-old when they first joined civic activities. Those involved at such a young age were engaged in fundraising, donations to charity, and so on. A handful of Mainland respondents reported participating in volunteering work, the Occupy Movement, and university matters.

Most respondents, local and Mainland, described themselves as only occasionally active in civic processes, or as not active. The key reason mentioned by local respondents was a busy life and academic work. A few also reported being warned by their parents to stay out of politics. Most Mainland respondents indicated they were not interested in politics and needed to focus on their studies, while a few who reported being occasionally active explained that they have few opportunities to participate in civic processes as the Chinese government prohibits them.

Respondents indicated mixed levels of support for the government type in Hong Kong. The largest percentage (44 %) of local respondents indicated they were neutral, while others were split for or against it (4 % stated they did not care). Among Mainland respondents, over half (53 %) were neutral, with most others (28 %) indicating they did not care. Among local respondents, some expressed doubt of the credibility and operations of the government and concerns with Chinese interference in local events. Those who were supportive expressed the system worked well and/or is balanced and largely representative. Among those from Mainland, many stated that they were not local residents and would not stay in Hong Kong after graduation, and/or were unfamiliar with the Hong Kong government.

When asked about the government type in Mainland China, most local respondents (61 %) were against it or not supportive, with just a few (23 %) supportive or very supportive (19 % neutral). Those against the Chinese government type noted it does not respect human rights. They felt the Communist Party dominates China, corruption is commonplace, and there is no democracy. Those who were neutral commented that they are not familiar with the Chinese government or otherwise found it difficult to make judgment. Among Mainland respondents, one-third were supportive, and one-third neutral, with less (14 %) not supportive. Those Mainland respondents who supported the government felt the government brought China into prosperity, while those who were neutral noted that another government type might not work better. Those who were not supportive stated the government has too much control and prohibits diverse voices.

When asked about democratic government in general, a slightly different picture emerged. Among local respondents, most (66 %) indicated they were supportive or very supportive, with the second largest group identifying as neutral (18 %). Among Mainland respondents, the largest group (44 %) was supportive or very supportive with one-third neutral. Among local (and some Mainland) students who indicated they were against democratic government, the comments reflected not a stance against democracy but challenges of implementation:

> It's not democratic, especially when a pro-Beijing loyalist has always been elected as Hong Kong Chief Executive. (student #409)

> Democratic governments don't really work either, too much filibustering. (student #474)

Those who were neutral also highlighted challenges of democratic governance. Those supportive discussed democracy as the best form of government or the best approach for accounting for diverse people's voices:

> Democracy is essential in improving a society. (student #368)

> It promotes freedom of expression and empowers people to have their own say in the community they are living in, which I think should be a natural right. We also see democratic governments thrive better than dictatorships around the world. (student #228)

Respondents were also asked to describe their ideal form of government. Common themes among local respondents included that all the citizens should participate in the government (40 %), representation (21 %), and descriptions of ideal traits of government leaders (10 %) such as being passionate, insightful, brave, caring, or willing to listen to and serve the public. Nearly all (local respondents commenting) stated representatives should be selected through voting, election, or universal suffrage. Among Mainland participants, many described the characteristics of government officials, such as that they are capable, well educated, and/or professional. Mainland respondents focused more on qualification, whereas local respondents mentioned people who strive for change, fight for justice, and listen to people. When asked about responsibilities of the government, local respondents indicated it should cater to the interests and needs of people, improve living standards and quality of life, listen to people's voices, and protect human rights. Among Mainland respondents, serving citizens and improving quality of life were mentioned most often, followed by national security and economic development.

Cross-Tab Analysis: Internal and External Factors

Cross-tab analysis demonstrates that both internal and external factors contribute to youth civic engagement. Demographic characteristics may shape youth civic behavior. The variable of gender demonstrates a positive impact on voting behavior but not on participation in public affairs. Personality also influences voting but not engagement in public affairs. Those who self-identified as expressive were more likely to vote. On the contrary, those who self-identified as analytical were less likely to vote, perhaps because they believe that voting cannot make a substantial difference under the current political system. Political attitudes also drive people to vote and participate in public affairs. Attitudes that are anti-government, pro-autonomy of Hong Kong, and for democracy push people to vote; the former two attitudes also encourage youth to engage in public affairs. Internal efficacy, which means one believes ordinary people can make a difference to the society, motivates participants to vote, but not to get involved in public affairs.

External factors such as civic education and political socialization both somewhat affect civic engagement of youth in Hong Kong. Civic education does not show any statistical impact on voting, but it inspires youth to take a greater part in public affairs. In addition, those who regard themselves as political knowledgeable, perhaps as a result of civic education, are significantly more likely to vote and participate in other civic duties. Students socialized politically in Hong Kong are more likely to participate in civic activities such as voting and other public affairs such as community work, charity, demonstration, and petition, compared to their counterparts from Mainland China, echoing the findings above. However, it seems that parents exert no strong influence on participants. Family political activism demonstrates no statistically significant effect on voting or other civic behavior, though its impact on public affairs engagement almost reaches the 0.05 statistical significance level.

Discussion

Researchers in Hong Kong and China have historically contrasted these societies in terms of civic education. While China has historically provided extensive patriotic nationalistic education to young people, which has been decried in the public sphere in Hong Kong in recent years as akin to "brainwashing" (EDB, 2012; Chou, 2012; Jackson, 2014), Hong Kong's experience of civic education has been described as piecemeal, ambivalent, and minimal (Fairbrother, 2003; Jackson, 2014; Lai & Byram, 2012; Vickers, 2005; Leung, 2008, Kapai, Bacon-Shone, Walsh, & Wong, 2014). An empirical analysis of curriculum supports this view, as in China, a formal curriculum for civic education is part of school timetables (and facilitated in other areas of life), while in Hong Kong, such a subject has been viewed with widespread mistrust and protest, as seen in the National Education controversy of 2012 (EDB, 2012; Chou, 2012). A review of human rights education in Hong Kong reveals that Hong Kong teachers are ill-equipped to teach the subject given confusion over concepts such as political freedoms and fears of loss of authority or control (Kapai et al., 2014). An assumption—backed up by Fairbrother (2003) and related polling of Hong Konger's public attitudes (Chung, 2016)—was that such disparities in terms of civic education had led to a depoliticized Hong Kong population (Lee, 2008), in contrast with a highly nationalist Mainland China.

However, our study finds that more Hong Kong youth than Mainland youth recollect their civic education in secondary schooling, and more Hong Kong youth found this education to be useful. In contrast to the picture imagined of brainwashed youth, Mainland respondents were highly critical of their political education, while Hong Kong students were more supportive (this echoes to some extent Fairbrother's findings related to the critical orientation of these two groups). Despite the lack of formalized civic education in Hong Kong, historically and today, most local respondents recalled learning civic education and reported finding it useful. The reported utility, however, may have been bolstered by recent local and university affairs. Our findings do reflect a generational gap in civic engagement, which aligns with the depoliticized civic education that was the norm before the Handover.

One only needs to pay attention to Hong Kong local or university politics today to observe that Hong Kong people are hardly the depoliticized subjects they have historically been represented as. Our survey gives a glimpse of what this means at the ground level for young people in Hong Kong today, who have been portrayed as central players in an era of heightened politicization where politics has pervaded nearly all spheres of life, including university appointments, curriculum, academic freedom, the use of Cantonese versus Mandarin dialects, and even street food stalls. Half the local respondents reported directly participating in public affairs in the past two years, and most of these respondents indicated their participation affected their views on politics and government as a powerful alternate source of informal civic education. Students' experiences in public affairs helped them learn about social and political issues firsthand, which triggered their reflection and evaluation of existing government policy.

During the recent protests and movements in Hong Kong, dissatisfaction and frustration toward the government were exacerbated, as youth experienced the government's ineffectiveness at responding to their requests and concerns. They also experienced the harshness of the government's response in some instances. Many have the night of September 28, 2014, etched into their memory as a dark episode in Hong Kong's history, which saw the police unleash 80 rounds of tear gas to disperse crowds staging an Occupy sit-in to demand universal suffrage in accordance with international norms. This spurred on an unprecedented wave of supporters to join the ranks of the movement, which went on for 79 days, ending in December 2014. Unsurprisingly, given Mainland China's lack of democracy and Mainland students' lack of long-term historical experience in Hong Kong, Mainland participants' engagement in public affairs was much lower.

Though hardly as apathetic as many youth are seen to be in western societies today, Hong Kong youth should not be typecast now as universally committed to civic engagement at the ground level; nor are they overly enthusiastic about what they hope to achieve in light of recent political events, the Umbrella Movement, and university-level politics. Indeed, the failure of the Umbrella Movement in terms of influencing a change in the Chinese government's policy toward Hong Kong's democratization has fueled a feeling of fatigue, helplessness, and despondence in some youth. For others, however, the disappointment coupled with an increasingly heavy-handed approach toward Hong Kong's affairs has strengthened their resolve to put up a fight. This has manifested itself in increased organized activity at the university level by student unions and groups to guard their core beliefs and values in the face of what they perceive to be a gradual encroachment into their autonomy and rights. Against this background, most local students were nonetheless only occasionally active, and close to half were inactive.

Finally, our findings reflect the traditional contrasts across the two groups other research has captured (Fairbrother, 2003; Lee, 2008) regarding views of democracy and of Mainland Chinese governance. Local respondents clearly support the Hong Kong type of government over that of Mainland China, while for the Mainland group, more showed support for China's government. One of the main reasons given by Mainland respondents was lack of familiarity with the local Hong Kong government.

In terms of democratic governance, most local respondents were favorable and supportive, while Mainland respondents were supportive or neutral. Taken as a whole, our findings reflect spirited and critical youth in Hong Kong and from Mainland China today, who are active and inquisitive, and realistic, if not also somewhat pessimistic. As future leaders of their society, they reflect a new wave of more engaged, active democratic participants. Time will tell how their visions will impact their societies, as they work for harmonization with each other as well as for better quality of life and personal liberty and prosperity across both systems in the future.

Conclusion

Our comparison of local and Mainland university students in Hong Kong suggests that student civic engagement may be influenced by education background (i.e., whether educated in Hong Kong or China), and that social and political views are shaped by experience in civic engagement processes. While local students care more about their freedom and rights, Mainland students tended to focus more on the basic needs of citizens. While local students have more opportunities to engage in protests or civic processes, their Mainland peers seldom have such opportunities, which are largely prohibited by the Chinese government. Although Mainland students are aware of the limitations of the Chinese government, they do not indicate a sense of opposition, as did some local respondents. On the other hand, our Mainland student group was quite small and less diverse and representative. More research should be conducted comparing Mainland youth living in Hong Kong from different backgrounds, as well as with those based in Mainland China.

Educational Recommendations

Our findings seem to support attitudes commonplace among the Hong Kong public that are ambivalent about civic education and suggest "less is more." As tension in society continues between those for and against systematic civic education, Hong Kong youth report learning substantively about the government in secondary schooling. Despite being typecast as dupes in the National Education controversy, Mainland youth participating in our survey did not show a blind sense of patriotic loyalty to Mainland China, while in both groups, some indicated that not all that they learned in school was useful in relation to their place in society.

One direction forward in this context would be to develop a more participatory sense of civic education in both contexts, that is, more student-centered and focused on what students can themselves do. On the other hand, if we take the voices of the engaged and critical youth represented in this study to heart, we might also critically ponder youth's capacity to make an impact, within a Mainland Chinese society which lacks a broader commitment to human rights and a Hong Kong that is undoubtedly experiencing a political identity crisis, accompanied by rising levels of public insecurity, distrust of the Mainland, and fear.

Meanwhile, students report learning about the government through their own civic engagements and public actions. As indicated in this study, this learning is not always pleasant but instead is often difficult, as participants reported feeling neglected by the government, or seeing their needs or those of the disadvantaged not heard at the public level. Yet as witnessed during the Umbrella Movement, youth are quick to learn on their feet how to collaborate and work together to solve problems when caught up in powerful transformative civic actions. This was best displayed by the culture of public sharing that developed at the sites of the Umbrella Movement, where citizens took turns taking the microphone to discuss issues of concern and educational communities were set up to facilitate student learning on site since they were missing classes, with experts invited to lecture students on themes pertaining to rule of law and human rights. Such education that is oriented toward experience and public impact can no doubt raise capacities for understanding and making positive democratic and other civic changes to society. This suggests that Liberal Studies (Jackson, 2014) and related moves toward experiential learning at the secondary and tertiary levels of education may be highly valuable to students, while more abstract learning about current and historical government structures may be less helpful in this era. *Learning by doing* may very well replace *learning to do* (CDC, 2009) in local educational strategies if youth civic engagement is to be prioritized in Hong Kong in the future.

NOTE

1. The authors wish to acknowledge the research support provided by the Education Policy Unit (EPU) of the Faculty of Education, University of Hong Kong.

REFERENCES

Chou, K. P. (2012). Hong Kong's national education controversy. *EAI Background Brief No. 753.*

Chung, R. T.-Y. (2016). *People's ethnic identity.* Hong Kong: University of Hong Kong public opinion programme. Retrieved from https://www.hkupop.hku.hk/english/popexpress/ethnic/index.html.

Curriculum Development Council (CDC). (2009). *Liberal studies curriculum guide.* Hong Kong: EB.

Curriculum Development Council (CDC). (2012). *Moral and national education curriculum guide.* Hong Kong: Education Bureau.

Education Bureau (EB). (2012). *Concerns and clarifications about 'steamrollering the implementation of moral and national education (MNE) by the government.* Hong Kong: EB.

Education Policy Unit (EPU). (2015). *Stories untold: What happened in schools during the occupy movement 2014?* Hong Kong: HK Association of the Heads of Secondary Schools/University of HK EPU.

Fairbrother, G. P. (2003). *Toward critical patriotism: Student resistance to political education in Hong Kong and China.* Hong Kong: University of HK Press.

Jackson, L. (2014). Who belongs in what Hong Kong? Citizenship education in the special administrative region. In J. E. Petrovic & A. M. Kuntz (Eds.), *Citizenship education around the world: Local contexts and global possibilities.* New York: Routledge.

Jackson, L. (2015). Religion in Hong Kong: Representation in liberal studies textbooks. *Asian Anthropology, 14*(1), 43–56.

Kapai, P. (2011). A principled approach towards judicial review: Lessons from *W v Registrar of Marriages. Hong Kong Law Journal, 41,* 49–75.

Kapai, P., Bacon-Shone, J., Walsh, S., & Wong, F. (2014). Children's rights education: International legal framework and state party obligations, Hong Kong Committee for UNICEF, *HKSAR v. Ng Kung Siu & Another* (1999) 2 HKCFAR 442.

Lai, P.-S., & Byram, M. (2012). *Re-shaping education for citizenship: Democratic national citizenship education in Hong Kong.* Newcastle upon Tyne: Cambridge Scholars Press.

Lam, J. T. M. (2015). Political decay in Hong Kong after the Occupy Central Movement. *Asian Affairs: An American Review, 42,* 99–121.

Lee, W. O. (2008). The development of citizenship education curriculum in Hong Kong after 1997: Tensions between national identity and global citizenship. In D. L. Grossman, W. O. Lee, & K. J. Kennedy (Eds.), *Citizenship curriculum in Asia and the Pacific.* Hong Kong: Comparative Education Research Centre/ Springer.

Leung, Y. W. (2008). An 'action-poor' human rights education: A critical review of the development of human rights education in the context of civic education in Hong Kong. *Intercultural Education, 19*(3), 231–242.

Leung, Y. W., & Ng, S. W. (2004). Back to square one: The re-depoliticizing of civic education in Hong Kong. *Asia Pacific Journal of Education, 24*(1), 43–60.

Ng Ka Ling v Director of Immigration [1999] 1 HKLRD 315.

Sweeting, A. (1992). Hong Kong education within historical processes. In G. A. Postiglione (Ed.), *Education and society in Hong Kong: Toward one country and two systems*. Hong Kong: University of HK Press.

Vickers, E. (2005). *In search of an identity: The politics of history as a school subject in Hong Kong, 1960–2005*. Hong Kong: Comparative Education Research Centre/University of HK.

CHAPTER 5

Citizenship Education Discourse(s) in India

Vanessa V. Tse and Catherine Broom

This chapter begins with a descriptive discussion of citizenship education in one region of India in order to present one way of thinking about citizenship. Then, the chapter describes the findings of a survey study of Indian youth's conceptions of, and actions, toward citizenship in a different region of India. The chapter ends with a discussion of the findings.

ONE FORM OF CITIZENSHIP EDUCATION
VANESSA V. TSE

Tucked within the Himalayas is the home and school of Sundara.[1] Cradled in the school's valley, numerous villages huddle together quietly while the main town throbs with activity. Tourists push into photo-ready poses, clusters of old men in wool suits and traditional hats perch on low benches, and locals haggle over cloth, vegetables, and all manner of household items.

V.V. Tse (✉)
Independent Scholar, India
e-mail: vanessavoyatse@gmail.com

C. Broom
Faculty of Education, University of British Columbia Okanagan,
Kelowna, BC, Canada

© The Author(s) 2017
C. Broom (ed.), *Youth Civic Engagement in a Globalized World*,
Palgrave Studies in Global Citizenship Education and Democracy,
DOI 10.1057/978-1-137-56533-4_5

Village life in India retains much of its traditional potency, even as it mingles with modern sensibilities. Ladies walk by in wool dresses that are secured with silver chains, colorful kerchiefs adorn their heads, and on their backs they carry baskets piled high with hay or twigs. Satellites, cars, and motorcycles abound, even as cows linger on the roadsides and popcorn kernels and chilies dry on squares of fabric. The sound of drumming flows down from the village temple on a daily basis and sometimes a Hindu altar is carried down the road by a procession of men. Frequently, the ladies take to their looms and weave shawls outside in the sunshine. Shepherds amble down the road, whistling and hooting in special intonations only their flocks understand.

I begin with a description of place, simply because where Sundara is situated is not the way most people envision India, and because of the potent reality of "Conscious-shaping space. Space-shaped consciousness" and how "a culture evolve[s] in place, and ... shape the building blocks of knowing" (Meyer, 2008, p. 220). I seek to depict a small pocket of India because each state in India possesses a distinct culture with a strong sense of regional identity, which includes a local language, style of dress, dances, and food. Oommen (2005) speaks to the multifaceted milieu:

> Most societies in the world today are culturally heterogeneous but no society is as heterogeneous as the Indian society which has several religions and numerous languages, not to speak of racial groups. As quantity makes for quality, the stupendous cultural heterogeneity of India makes its society extremely complex. (p. 16)

India is an immensely stratified society (Ghosh, 2015, p. 33) where the formidable influence of caste is still felt. It is a subcontinent that contains multiple nations, a trio of sovereign states, and 23 officially recognized languages (Oommen, 2005).

Additionally, Jainism, Sikhism, Buddhism, and Hinduism were brought forth on Indian soil. It is imperative to recognize religion if one is to even vaguely comprehend Indian society. Hinduism is the dominant faith, followed by Islam and Christianity in terms of the number of adherents, but there are also multitudes of Jains, Buddhists, and Sikhs (Census of India, 2001). A slim 0.6 % of the population are aligned with an "other" religion, (it is probable this pertains to those connected to their Indigenous beliefs and the Bahá'í Faith) and remarkably, only 0.1 % identified as being affiliated with an unstated religion (Census of India, 2001). Indian society is informed by and embedded in a spiritual way of knowing. Mani (2009) articulates that, "the principal that animates this cultural matrix is a non-materialistic one. Most in our society accept the existence of a wider reality, and it is in this context that the meaning of life, success or poverty is interpreted" (p. 57).

While my description above speaks to the resplendent beauty of India, I have also witnessed devastating suffering: entire communities living in crumbling shacks atop mounds of garbage which they sift through for daily work; maimed and disfigured vagrants relegated to a life of begging; and children with dusty hair performing cartwheels beside rickshaws or lying in the streets with eyes half-closed in hunger. There is an open wound in India that cannot be evaded.

Countless people are locked in *poverty traps*, which posit them in situations of scarcity through factors outside their control or influence (Carpenter & Brock, 2008). The Hindu caste system exacerbates poverty through its enforcement of a hierarchy trap (Berkes & Folke, 2002). This perpetuates systemic oppression for those born into lower-ranking castes or those who are without caste, known as the Dalits or the "Untouchables." According to a 2011 census, there are approximately 201 million Dalits in India (Sivakumar, 2013).

A 2010 United Nations report ascertained that a third of the people surviving in extreme poverty, designated as those living on less than $1.25 a day, are Indian (UN, 2014). There is persistent hunger, under nutrition, and high childhood mortality in India, and many of these indexes are among the worst worldwide (Gaiha, Kulkarni, Pandey, & Imai, 2012). Twenty-five percent of the globe's undernourished people and more than a third of all underweight children are in India (UN, 2015). There is a need to care for the millions of India's vulnerable children.

Sundara

Sundara is a home that cares for and educates children from desperate circumstances. It provides children with all basic necessities, including clothing, food, education, and housing. Additionally, youth at Sundara are flourishing in all dimensions of life: spiritually, physically, emotionally, and mentally.

The home is founded and entirely run by Indian people who are dedicated to serving their community. There are two groups of children who attend the school located on site: those who board at the home, as well as "day scholars" who come for regular school hours and are admitted if they are from impoverished families in the village (and hence would most likely not be able to afford to attend school elsewhere). If there are any superfluous seats available at the school, then other families can seek admission. The school has garnered an exceptional reputation in the local village and surrounding communities. Indeed, so many parents seek to enroll their children that the principal collects the names of all interested parties and performs a draw. Those who are permanent residents of Sundara often return to and visit their biological families during their three-month winter break (unless their families are unable to receive them). No child is forced to reside at Sundara, and they may leave at any time.

It is clearly articulated to parents that the school will be teaching a Christian belief system. The children are expected to respectfully participate in the spiritual practices of the home; this includes devotional periods, attending church and prayer. However, other children's homes in India are situated in different religious views, and parents have selected Sundara for their own particular reasons.

Youth attend the school from kindergarten to grade eight, and many of the staff work in dual roles as both teachers and caregivers. Only the kindergarten and grade one students have a single teacher, all other learners have their classes divided by subjects.

One distinctive aspect of the school is the holistic way of learning and living that permeates life. Sundara is first and foremost a family with rich layers of reciprocal relationships between the staff, didis and bhaiyas (older sisters and brothers), and friends (those in the children's peer group). The way of living and being at Sundara is very much in line with the purpose of holistic education, which is deeply grounded in a focus on relationships and the fullest development of each learner.

Holistic educators are attentive to the spirit, emotions, mind, and body of each individual (J. Miller, 2010[2]); the foundation of this form of education is rooted in the ideologies of connectedness and interdependence (Mahmoudi, Jafari, Nasrabadi, & Liaghatdar, 2012). Holistic education invites educators to cultivate relationships with others, oneself, and the earth (Cajete, 1994; J. Miller 2006, 2007, 2010; J. Miller & Seller, 1990; Palmer, 1983/1993). Furthermore, the holistic education paradigm is not concerned with replicating citizens who will become successful in the way qualified by dominant society (Roszak, 1978), where such success is defined in material and economic terms (Mani, 2009; R. Miller, 1990). Sundara undoubtedly seeks for all its graduates to be able to support themselves financially (all who board there are provided with the means to pursue a university education). Yet, the successful graduates celebrated by the home are those who not only completed post-secondary education, but also have gone on to serve their communities. This includes one individual who uses his expertise in commerce to teach impoverished youth basic financial skills to manage funds and another graduate who opened her own children's home that also cares for vulnerable children. As well, the current director of Sundara was herself brought up by the home.

Schools and Citizenship Education

Schools in India, like many in the west, are partitioned into public (government schools) and private spheres. Unfortunately, schools in rural communities "generally represent miserable lack of infrastructures such as inadequate number of teachers, textbooks, classrooms and other amenities vis-a-vis high student population, which seriously affect the quality of education" (Ghosh, 2015, p. 33). Hence, many families strive to provide their children with private education. Sundara could technically be qualified as a private school, but with a population dissimilar to most in this category.

In the state in which Sundara is located, the curriculum encompasses math, drawing, writing, science, Hindi, Sanskrit, computers, English, and social studies. The social studies curriculum is divided into three sections: civics, geography, and history. I turn now to an examination of the civics curriculum as it is taught at Sundara.

The state curriculum is administered not through curricular documents, but rather through textbooks. I examined many of the textbooks to better understand their proposed learning outcomes. Young children begin by learning about their neighborhood (Gupta, 2013), and in grade four, they are introduced to local self-government and elections (Roy & Jain, 2013). In grade five, the children are familiarized with India's colonial history and the struggle for freedom led by Gandhi; students learn about *satyagraha*, non-violence, and non-cooperation (Roy & Jain, 2009). The grade five curriculum emphasizes the influence of women, highlighting their contributions in religious and social reforms and garnering independence from the British (Roy & Jain, 2009). Students concentrate on the rights and duties of citizenship in grades five and seven. The sixth grade curriculum is more focused on Indian government structures and communities. There is a particularly holistic notion in the latter aforementioned curriculum in the importance placed on interdependence and cooperation (Sengupta,

2013). Democracy is emphasized and students learn about various political systems, parties, and voting.

One of the teachers surprised me with the phrase: *unity in diversity.* Oommen (2005) further alerted me to this concept and its manifestation in the Indian context: "the celebration of its cultural diversity as a fact and the nurturing of its cultural pluralism as a value are the birthmarks of India" (p. 18). I previously discussed the amount of heterogeneity in India (which is also taught in the local curriculum) and I found myself wondering what is it that unites India? This is particularly pertinent because a crucial issue for nation-states globally is how to construct a shared national identity while legitimizing and recognizing difference (Banks, 2008). In another conversation with one of the teachers on this subject, she noted that there is *something* that connects them across boundaries. When I inquired into what exactly that something is, she immediately responded, "We are one." She directed me to the curriculum, which provided me with a fascinating elucidation on the national identity of India:

> Beneath all the bewildering and complex disparities in India there is an underlying unity. What unites these diverse communities is our national identity. We are all, first and foremost, Indians. The ties that bind us are deep emotional bonds, that instill in us a sense of oneness or Indianness. This spirit of oneness is essentially a collective, group memory of past achievements, traditions and experiences. (Sengupta, 2013, pp. 134–135)

Indians appear to share a communal resoluteness in maintaining disparate regional identities, and their commitment to this is unifying. Furthermore, the nature of the Indian national identity has an affective timbre, as "the forms through which national identity is appropriated and expressed are often as much emotional as they are conceptually elaborated" (Gates, 2006, p. 572).

The students of Sundara have citizenship education modeled to them through the exemplary model of Amaley.[3] This form of citizenship education is aligned with Broom's (2010) notion that "caring for others and for our planet, and manifesting this care through action, is citizenship. Supporting exploited people around the world to live lives with dignity is citizenship" (p. 150). All life at Sundara is imbued with a distinctly holistic hue, and this extends to citizenship education, which is not relegated just to the social studies curriculum but extends into other facets of life. However, the staff would not call this citizenship education; it would be seen as part of the children's moral, spiritual, and social development.

Amaley is the founder of Sundara, and in her "retirement" is still a force to be reckoned with. She lives on site and is involved in daily life. Amaley currently runs a vocational center for disadvantaged women, which provides training in sewing and computers so that the women can obtain skills to seek future employment. This center is also the base for disaster relief efforts. After a fire devastated a local village, Amaley organized relief efforts, fundraised, and distributed these goods to those affected.

Amaley is also politically involved and is regarded as a holy woman and a local Mother Teresa. In the recent election of the village head, she led her own campaign. Amaley did not run for office, nor did she try to garner votes for any particular candidate. Rather, she focused her efforts on trying to help the local people understand important matters on which to vote. Amaley urged people to consider candidates who would attend to the following issues: environmental concerns, pertaining to water supplies and protecting their forest; and focusing on the needs of all village people, especially the poor and sick. She encouraged others to cast their votes for someone who was not corrupt; and finally, someone who would give their time to all the people, and not discriminate against the poor. Amaley spoke at a village meeting and put up posters outlining these topics in 30 other villages.

Amaley has changed hundreds of lives. In the realm of citizenship education, her work is important, because students "learn much from schools, but what they learn is not only in their lessons. Teachers and administrators must learn to model the skills we want students to develop" (UN Global Education First Initiative, 2012). Part of the educational experience is the teacher—who he or she *is* (Forbes, 2012). To truly teach citizenship education, and for that matter, to teach holistically, teachers must embody such practices in their own lives because the teacher is the teaching (Aoki, 1992) and "We teach who we are" (Palmer, 1998).

The education and way of life at the home, as previously noted, is deeply holistic. This is felt even on the level of citizenship education where children not only learn about citizenship, but also have an exemplary model who embodies the best of what is possible in a member of society. The children are also given opportunities to volunteer in the community. The ability to care results from the care an individual has received (Broom, 2010) and in this way, it is no surprise that many of the graduates of Sundara have gone on to live lives dedicated to service and the betterment of their communities.

RESEARCH STUDY: SURVEYS

Trying to get a sense of how youth in this diverse nation feel is challenging. Thus, the authors described one unique location above. In addition, Indian youth in New Delhi were invited to participate in a survey study in public places in the city in the spring 2015. The youth filled out anonymous surveys online, which collected the same information as the Canadian survey.

Limitations of Study Findings

The researchers hoped to carry out the survey study with youth across India in varied socioeconomic categories and varied post-secondary educational programs and careers. However, the youth who participated cannot be considered to be representative of all youth in India: we are given only a sample of how some youth feel. As in other nations, participation of youth remained limited. Further, while some scholars in India showed interest in participating in the study, financial and logistical challenges made it difficult for the scholars to complete the study. The few youth who filled out the survey were generally youth who came from middle or high income homes who had internet access at home and were fluent in English (Table 5.1).

All the youth in New Delhi who participated in the online survey were males, between the ages of 20 and 26. They identified their citizenship as Indian, and their first languages as Hindi or Punjabi. Most (83 %) stated they had studied citizenship education in school. They stated that they found it useful as they learned about government processes:

> Makes us understand the working of political system. (student #3)

> because it educates us about the rights and duties of a good citizen and government. (student #6)

The youth identified themselves as having some knowledge of, or of being knowledgeable of, government processes. All stated that they followed the news, mostly online, from science and sports news to national and international news, due to interest:

> I am interested in my country's politics and what other countries are doing. (student #5).

Table 5.1   India: Summary of research findings

Indian youth	Number of participants: 6			
Demographics				
Gender	Male: 100 %	Female: 0 %	Other/Undisclosed:0 %	
Cultural Identification	Indian: 100 %		Other: 0 %	
First Language	Hindi: 83 %	Punjabi: 17 %	Other: 0 %	
	Yes	No	Do not remember	
Citizenship education	83 %	17 %	0 %	
	Knowledgeable	Some knowledge	Lack knowledge	
Political knowledge	50 %	50 %	0 %	
	Yes	No	Unsure	
Follow the news	100 %	0 %	0 %	
Personal political experience	83 %	17 %	0 %	
Family's political involvement	67 %	33 %	0 %	
Personality type	Assertive	Amiable	Humanistic	Analytical
	16 %	30 %	0 %	16 %
	Important	Quite important	Not important	
Attitude to community engagement	100 %	0 %	0 %	
Attitude to political participation	100 %	0 %	0 %	
	Effective	Somewhat effective	Ineffective	
Level of personal efficacy	83 %	17 %	0 %	
	Active	Somewhat active	Inactive	
Civic involvement	33 %	67 %	0 %	
	Supportive	Neutral	Do not care/not supportive	
Attitudes toward democracy	50 %	50 %	0 %	
Attitude toward govt. system in India	40 %	20 %	40 %	

(*continued*)

Table 5.1   (continued)

Indian youth	Number of participants: 6		
Students' civic participation (Top 3)	Yes	No	No response
Donating money to causes	100 %	0 %	0 %
Helping those in need	100 %	0 %	0 %
Being a good neighbor	100 %	0 %	0 %
Granting citizenship (Top three)			
Being interested in the common wellbeing			
Having work			
Paying taxes			

Most (83 %) stated that they had had a significant political experience. They described issues with government instability or corruption:

> Indian political system is corrupt and totally erratic. Mishaps keep occurring every now and then. (student #2)

> Due to corruption at a major level. (student #3)

Most (67 %) also stated that their families had been active when they were growing up, primarily by voting. Half stated that their parents were Liberal in their political views, and most (83 %) stated that they were Liberal in their beliefs. They described their personality types as amiable, leader, introverted, or mixed type and felt that good citizens should be patriotic, intelligent, respectful, and "take part in nation building" (student #6). All the youth felt that it was important for people to participate in their communities, as it would lead to improvements:

> Basic necessity for development and harmony. (student #3)

All the youth felt that they could be effective (83 %) or somewhat effective (17 %) in their actions. They stated:

> Because I feel there should be a change and someone should take the initiative to implement it. (student #2)

> I have seen some people affecting the society through small deeds. (student #5)

Their top free time activities were: sports (100 % of respondents), spending time with friends (100 %), and interacting with social media (100 %). Most (83 %) stated they were involved in patriotic activities, many (67 %) were involved in politics through discussions or other means. Half stated they were involved in community work. Only one person was active in religious activities. For their civic activities, all (100 %) stated that they donated money to causes, helped those in need, and were a good neighbor. Most (83 %) voted and followed political news. Few (16 %) were involved in more active political activities such as boycotting, joining a political party, or writing government officials.

All of the youth were active or occasionally active. They stated that time limited their engagement and that they got involved in areas of their interest:

> Out of my interests whenever I have time, I get involved. (student #5)

They had varied attitudes to their government in India, with even numbers being for and again the government and one being neutral. The youth stated concerns over government corruption and religious intolerance. One youth wrote:

> Current government is trying to provide jobs and hence food and livings compared to previous congress government whose policies was always provide free stuff to people and earn their votes which crippled our nation's economy. (student #6)

The youth were more supportive of the concept of democracy in general with 50 % supporting democracy and 50 % being neutral. While some commented on corruption, they also stated that democracy was the best option:

> its for the people, by the people. (student #3)

> every leader is corrupt it's just that we have to choose less one. They try to influence people on the basis of castes and religion. (student #6)

All the youth (100 %) felt that people should participate politically in their society, stating that people should be active for the good of the community, for equality, and in order to bring change. They stated that their ideal government would be run by the public and not be partisan or corrupt. They believed that the main characteristics a citizen of the country should have were: being interested in the common wellbeing, having work and paying taxes (83 % of respondents chose these), followed by being born in the nation and being a good neighbor (67 %). Only one respondent felt that citizens should share the same lifestyle. In other chapters, we carried out cross-tabs analysis in order to consider correlations between internal and external factors and youth's civic attitudes and behaviors. However, this sample is too small to be able to carry out such an analysis. We describe what correlations appear in the data in a general sense.

Internal Factors

In this survey, only males filled out the survey, and personality types were mixed. As to attitudes, youth who were supportive, neutral, or not supportive of their government, all voted. Further, all the youth stated that it was important for people to participate politically in their nation, and all stated that they were occasionally active or active. Like in Canada, an attitude of valuing participation was associated with active participation. It may also be that having some sort of attitude of engagement toward one's government, whether positive or not, can lead to active participation.

External Factors

External factors may also influence youth's civic attitudes and behaviors. All the youth who stated that they had studied citizenship education in school also stated they voted. The youth who stated he had not studied citizenship education in schools was occasionally active in social forms of citizenship such as giving money or volunteering and not political forms. Youth who stated that their families were or were not active participated in civic processes; however, all of the youth who stated that their parents voted, also stated they voted. All the youth who stated they had had a significant experience also all voted. Like in Canada, it seems that youth are more active and vote if their parents vote, the youth have studied citizenship education, and they have had significant a political experience.

DISCUSSION

The educated, urban youth in New Delhi who filled out the surveys responded much like Canadian youth: most stated that they had studied citizenship education in school, felt knowledgeable of politics, followed the news, and felt their actions mattered. They were involved in traditional civic activities, such as voting, volunteering, or donating money. All the youth felt that citizens should be actively involved in their society. They demonstrated a varied attitude to the government in India, describing issues with corruption, and a more positive orientation to the concept of democracy. Like Canadian youth, they mentioned distrust of politicians. They believed citizens should be interested in the common wellbeing and contribute to society by working and paying taxes. More youth stated that citizens should be born in the country than young Canadians did, although like young Canadians, they did not feel that youth had to share the same lifestyles as them. This openness, along with attention to the common wellbeing, may connect to the conception of holistic citizenship described above. Youth in Canada and India share similar connections between various key factors associated with citizenship, including attitudes, citizenship education, families, personal experiences, and civic/political behaviors.

Closing Thoughts, Vanessa V. Tse

There is an enduring need to transform the core of many educational communities (Abbott, 2010; Freire, 2005; hooks, 2003; O'Sullivan, 2002), and citizenship education plays a critical role in such transformation in the face of global dilemmas. Education is not just an instrument for transformation, but an organic and integral aspect of ushering in a new way of being (Tse & Monk, 2015). It is heartening to speak of those who embody what can be achieved in education, leaning into the complexities of teaching and learning with intention and courage (Tanaka & Tse, 2015).

CONCLUSION

How can contextual factors, such as poverty, and cultural considerations, such as caste, be addressed to expand citizenship education opportunities to diverse youth? This chapter seems to illustrate a conception of citizenship that is found in common among well-educated youth in diverse places, yet similar social spaces. This conception can be considered to be one of the "globalized elite class" (Bauman, 2000), free to transverse and shape the world.

This chapter provides us with a glimpse of how the care of some for others found in challenging contexts opens new possibilities for citizenship and citizenship education. This education can become a lived disposition that aims to help others in the community, initiating a humanist cycle that builds citizenship as a sense of humanity and compassion for others. It is clear that how citizenship education is understood and taught, and the context it occurs within, relates to how youth can come to live their own citizenship. Citizenship and its related citizenship education are a discourse that can come to structure youth's perceptions and actions. Currently, many nation-states promote a discourse of citizenship and citizenship education as political knowledge of government structures and processes that includes a disposition to value democracy and participate through means such as voting. This is the disposition that youth in diverse nations who share a common life in terms of their education, life interests, and careers seem to come to embrace. In this chapter, we read of another possible discourse in which citizenship is a sense of care, humanity, and compassion for others. We have opportunities to consider different ways of thinking about what citizenship is and entails, with lived consequences.

NOTES

1. All names related to and including Sundara are pseudonyms that have been altered for the purposes of anonymity.
2. In holistic education, John P. Miller and Ron Miller are two distinguished scholars, to differentiate between the pair, I use their first initials in all in-text citations.
3. Amaley is a title that translates to *great mother*.

REFERENCES

Abbott, J. (2010). *Overschooled but undereducated: How the crisis in education is jeopardizing our adolescents*. London: Continuum International.

Aoki, T. (1992). Layered voices of teaching: The uncannily correct and the elusively true. In W. F. Pinar & W. M. Reynolds (Eds.), *Understanding curriculum as phenomenological and deconstructed text* (pp. 17–27). New York: Teachers College Press.

Banks, J. A. (2008). Diversity, group identity, and citizenship education in a global age. *Educational Researcher, 37*(3), 129–139.

Bauman, Z. (2000). *Globalization the human consequences*. New York: Columbia University Press.

Berkes, F., & Folke, C. (2002). The Hindu caste system and the hierarchy trap. In L. H. Gunderson & C. S. Holling (Eds.), *Panarchy: Understanding transformations in human and natural systems* (pp. 97–98). Washington, DC: Island Press.

Broom, C. (2010). Conceptualizing and teaching citizenship as humanity. *Citizenship, Social and Economics Education, 9*(3), 147–155.

Cajete, G. (1994). *Look to the mountain: An ecology of indigenous education*. San Francisco: Kivaki Press.

Carpenter, S. R., & Brock, W. A. (2008). Adaptive capacity and traps. *Ecology and Society, 13*(2), 40.

Census of India. (2001). *Religion*. Retrieved from http://censusindia.gov.in/Census_And_You/religion.aspx

Forbes, S. H. (2012). Holistic education: Its nature and intellectual precedents. *Encounter: Education for Meaning and Social Justice, 25*(2), 1–330.

Freire, P. (1970/2005). *Pedagogy of the oppressed* (M. B. Ramos, Trans.). New York: The Continuum International Publishing Group.

Gaiha, R., Kulkarni, V., Pandey, M., & Imai, K. (2012). On hunger and child mortality in India. *Journal of Asian and African Studies, 47*(1), 3–17.

Gates, B. E. (2006). Religion as cuckoo or crucible: Beliefs and believing as vital for citizenship and citizenship education. *Journal of Moral Education, 35*(4), 571–594.

Ghosh, S. (2015). Learning from community: Agenda for citizenship education. *Education, Citizenship and Social Justice, 10*(1), 21–36.

Gupta, V. (2013). *Trek: Primary social studies book 2* (2nd ed.). New Delhi, India: Oxford University Press.

hooks, b. (2003). *Teaching community: A pedagogy of hope*. New York: Routledge.

Mahmoudi, S., Jafari, E., Nasrabadi, H. A., & Liaghatdar, M. J. (2012). Holistic education: An approach for 21 century. *International Education Studies, 5*(2), 178–186.

Mani, L. (2009). *SacredSecular: Contemplative cultural critique*. New Delhi, India: Routledge.

Meyer, M. A. (2008). Indigenous and authentic: Hawaiian epistemology and the triangulation of meaning. In N. K. Denzin, Y. S. Lincoln, & L. T. Smith (Eds.), *Handbook of critical and indigenous methodologies* (pp. 217–232). Thousand Oaks, CA: Sage.

Miller, R. (1990). *What are schools for? Holistic education in American culture*. Brandon, VT: Holistic Education Press.

Miller, J. P. (2006). *Educating for wisdom and compassion: Creating conditions for timeless learning*. Thousand Oaks, CA: Corwin Press.

Miller, J. P. (2007). *The holistic curriculum* (2nd ed.). Toronto, ON: University of Toronto Press Inc.

Miller, J. P. (2010). *Whole child education*. Toronto, ON: University of Toronto Press Inc.

Miller, J., & Seller, W. (1990). *Curriculum perspectives and practice*. Mississauga, ON: Copp Clark Pitman Ltd.

O'Sullivan, E. (2002). The project and vision of transformative education: Integral transformative learning. In E. O'Sullivan, A. Morrell, & M. A. O'Connor (Eds.), *Expanding the boundaries of transformative learning* (pp. 1–12). New York: Palgrave.

Oommen, T. K. (2005). *Crisis and contention in Indian society*. New Delhi, India: Sage Publications.

Palmer, P. J. (1983/1993). *To know as we are known: A spirituality of education*. San Francisco: HarperSanFrancisco.

Palmer, P. J. (1998). *The courage to teach: Exploring the inner landscape of a teacher's life*. San Francisco: Jossey-Bass.

Roszak, T. (1978). *Person/planet: The creative disintegration of industrialized society*. Lincoln, NE: iUniverse.

Roy, V., & Jain, R. (2009). *Trek: Primary social studies for class 5*. New Delhi, India: Oxford University Press.

Roy, V., & Jain, R. (2013). *Trek: Primary social studies for class 4* (2nd ed.). New Delhi, India: Oxford University Press.

Sengupta, J. (2013). *The trail 6: History and civics for ICSE middle school*. New Delhi, India: Oxford University Press.

Sivakumar, B. (2013, May 2). Half of India's dalit population lives in 4 states. *The Times of India*. Retrieved from http://timesofindia.indiatimes.com

Tanaka, M., & Tse, V. V. (2015). Touching the inexplicable: Poetry as transformativeinquiry. *Journal of Curriculum Theorizing, 30*(3), 45–62.

Tse, V. V., & Monk, D. F. (2015). Learning to be: Emerging discourse in awakening transformation in education. *In Education, 21*(1), 114–129.

UN Global Education First Initiative. (2012). *Priority # 3: Foster global citizenship*. Retrieved from http://www.globaleducationfirst.org/220.htm

United Nations. (2014). *Millennium development goals report*. Retrieved from http://in.one.un.org/page/latest-reports.

United Nations. (2015). *India and the MDGs: Towards a sustainable future for all*. Retrieved from http://in.one.un.org/page/latest-reports

CHAPTER 6

The Contradictory Place of Civic Education in the Italian Education System

Enzo Colombo

Currently, in many Western societies, young people are often depicted as 'lacking'. Most media, political discourses and social research tend to describe them as characterized by *uncertainty*—towards the future, personal relationships and professional tracks (Bauman, 1995; Beck, 1992; Means, 2015), *disinterest*—towards politics and public life (Jowell & Park, 1998; Kimberlee, 1998; Macedo, Alex-Assenhoh, & Berry, 2005; Putnam, 2000) and *resignation*—accepting the status quo without striking forms of protest, dissent or rebellion (Arthur & Davies, 2008; Beaumont, 2010; Harris, Wyn, & Youness, 2010; Levine, 2007).

Others are more optimistic and depict young people as 'active'. They suggest we are experiencing changing patterns of young adults' presence in civic life, rather than declining civic engagement. They observe that despite their reduced political life, young adults are often engaged in forms of 'alternative behavior' (volunteerism, online activism, participation in consumer activism, support of global causes and organization of protests and street performances) expressing new ways of civic engagement (Bennet,

E. Colombo (✉)
Dipartimento di Scienze sociali e politiche, University of Milan,
via Conservatorio, 7, 20122 Milan, Italy
e-mail: enzo.colombo@unimi.it

© The Author(s) 2017
C. Broom (ed.), *Youth Civic Engagement in a Globalized World*,
Palgrave Studies in Global Citizenship Education and Democracy,
DOI 10.1057/978-1-137-56533-4_6

103

2007; Melo & Stockemer, 2014; Sloam, 2014; Zaff, Boyd, Li, Lerner, & Lerner, 2010; Zukin, Keeter, Andolina, Jenkins, & Delli Carpini, 2006).

This ambivalent picture is particularly striking in Italy. Media and public opinion currently depict young people as both politically disengaged, passive and individualist and as new political actors able to overcome an old, bribed and ineffective ruling class, bringing new values and ethical commitments into the withered Italian political system and ageing Italian society. Young people catalyse both fears and hopes in a moment of great uncertainty, characterized by an economic crisis that mainly affects the lower and middle class of the population. Whether they are seen as a threat to the stability of the social cohesion and democracy or as a hope for renewal, politicians, opinion makers and scholars put strong emphasis on an urgent need for strengthening youth civic engagement, supporting youth active citizenship and developing effective programs of citizenship education.

In Italy, the debate about citizenship education and the role schools should play to make young people better-engaged citizens is long lasting. It has its roots in an unresolved tension between civic education and moral education.

Since its birth, in 1861, the Italian state has faced the issue of finding a balanced relation with the Catholic Church. In fact, the Italian state was instituted against the temporal power of the Catholic Church. Not to exacerbate the conflict and not to interfere with the moral convictions of a majority Catholic population, the emerging unified Italian state took upon itself the task of 'nation building' (with a strong emphasis on the values of nation and country), leaving the Catholic Church the monopoly of moral education in the private sphere. This defined a separation between the public sphere (the domain of the state, but limited to the strengthening of social cohesion) and privacy (the place of the formation of the 'moral character' and the deep values, realm of the Church). In this separation, the state (public school) did not have a decisive role in the moral education of citizens, limiting itself to instilling a patriotic spirit (Cavalli & Deiana, 1999). The aim of civic education was to convey feelings of national belonging to generations who struggled to recognize the state built in 1861. The conflict between the State and the Church marks a break between civic education and moral education. The first is the duty of the state and aims to build the citizen. The emphasis is on the objective-institutional dimension, and civic education is limited to 'train' young people on the functioning of the state and provide knowledge and respect of rules and laws. The second is left to the Church (or the family) and aims to build the person. The emphasis is on the subjective-existential dimension, and its main goal is to 'educate' young people to ethical and moral values.

A second historical experience marks the marginality of citizenship education in the Italian school system: the experience of fascism. On the one hand, fascism exacerbated the transmission of nationalist ideology; on the other hand, it used the school as a means to disseminate fascist ideology. At the same time, however, fascism kept intact the monopoly of the Catholic Church in the private sphere of ethics. The aim of civic education was to inculcate the principles of fascist ideology and military culture in the population, to ensure the full support of young people to the totalitarian regime and widespread control of the state on citizens' lives (Cavalli & Deiana, 1999).

After World War II and the proclamation of the Italian Republic (1946), the tension between the three different souls, which had given birth to the Resistance against fascism (the socialist–communist, the liberal–democratic, and the Catholic), has not allowed the state to assume a strong role in the transmission of shared civic values. Lacking a strong consensus on the role of the state and the ethical-political values underpinning the new democratic life, it was difficult to develop clear, effective and consistent educational programs on the basis of which to direct the education of young future citizens.

Civic education made its official entry into the Italian school in 1958 with a course of two hours per month, assigned to the history teacher. The main contents of the course consisted of a reasoned reading of the Constitution and the values that underpin it. From this moment on, civic education was confined, for a long period, to 'training' young people to learn norms, constitutional rules, and the functioning of institutions as an appendix of history or law. It focused on the knowledge and understanding of formal institutions and processes of civic life (such as voting in the elections, respecting the law, knowing and respecting the rules of the road and acting as a good neighbour).

THE EFFECTS OF EUROPEAN UNIFICATION AND GLOBALIZATION PROCESSES

Starting in the 1980s, Italy changed from an emigration country to an immigration one. The effects of being part of the European Union became more evident, promoting a closer convergence of the functioning of the state and the educational system among European countries.

Finally, globalization processes brought to the fore new issues, stimulating new form of belonging and identification, and put on the agenda the need for a new definition of citizenship. Civic education started to take account of ecological and environmental issues, human rights enhancement, global solidarity, multiculturalism and interculturalism.

The latest school reform in Italy (2010) has changed the name and contents of the teaching of civic education. A new course of one hour a week has been introduced, named 'Citizenship and Constitution'. It is part of the teaching of history and geography and includes five topics: environmental education, road safety education (knowledge of traffic laws), health education (basic knowledge of first aid), food education and the Italian Constitution. The new course, taking into account the directives of the European Recommendation of 2006 on key competences for lifelong learning, aims to prepare students to become active citizens, by ensuring that they have the necessary knowledge, skills and attitudes to contribute to the development and well-being of the society in which they live. In 2010, a new Council of Europe's Recommendation stressed the importance of an 'experience-based learning' of active citizenship, highlighting that 'one of the fundamental goals of all education for democratic citizenship and human rights education is not just equipping learners with knowledge, understanding and skills, but also empowering them with the readiness to take action in society in the defence and promotion of human rights, democracy and the rule of law' (CM/REC(2010)7).[1]

Although inspired by European suggestions, the new Italian course still focuses on training rather than education. Italy's citizenship education legacy is still evident, and school programs privilege teaching and learning the formal and juridical aspect of duties and rights in the classroom rather than stimulating practical experiences gained through school life and activity in wider society. The idea that school has to train rather than educate young people to become citizens is deeply rooted in teachers' attitudes. An European survey (Schulz, Ainley, Fraillon, Kerr, & Losito, 2010) analysing teachers' views on the importance of specific aims for civic and citizenship education highlights that Italian teachers consider the teaching of formal knowledge most important (well above the average percentages of their colleagues from other European countries), rather than stimulating concrete experiences. Half of them (European average: 31 %) consider civic and citizenship education related to knowledge of social, political and civic institutions as important; more than three out of four (European average: 63 %) give importance to knowledge of citizens' rights and responsibilities. On the other hand, only 8 % of them (European average: 15 %) consider participation in local community important, and only 11 % (European average: 19 %) regard participation in school life as a way to promote citizenship education (Education, Audiovisual and Culture Executive Agency, EACEA Eurydice, 2012).

Studies analysing youth active participation in the community (Ainley, Friedman, Kerr, & Schulz, 2012; Istituto Giuseppe Toniolo, 2013; Schulz et al., 2010) draw a similar picture. Italian youngsters are more likely to vote in both national and local elections than their European peers, while they are less engaged in more practical and community-oriented activities such as campaigning for a cause, doing something to help the community and collecting money for a social cause. Compared with their European peers, Italian youngsters are also less interested in voting or becoming a candidate for class representative and school parliament (EACEA Eurydice, 2012).

In summary, citizenship education in Italian schools is more concerned to promote the acquisition of formal knowledge about rules, laws and the functioning of the state rather than to stimulate active participation. It is no coincidence that community service has no formal recognition in Italy as a pedagogical strategy to promote active citizenship. This does not mean that education for active citizenship is absent from latent and informal curricula. Teachers and students are frequently engaged in promoting extra-curricular activities—often related to specific local projects and activities—but such activities remain based on individual initiatives and they are unequally distributed among schools. In fact, they are more frequent in the North of the country and in Lyceum,[2] while they are few and sporadic in the South and in vocational schools (Professional Institute).

DATA AND METHODS

The findings presented in this chapter are based on an online survey given out to Italian young people in the Fall of 2015. The 146 participants—aged between 18 and 29 years—were recruited by snowball sampling. All participated in the survey on a voluntary basis, no monetary reward or material was expected. The anonymous questionnaires included both closed- and open-ended questions. The questionnaire was advertised among the students of the Faculty of Political Science at the University of Milan and in different schools in Milan and the province, in both high and vocational schools. Participants in the survey were asked to invite other acquaintances to take part in the research. In addition, two focus groups were conducted with 14 students—aged between 18 and 23 years—attending a vocational school in Milan, North of Italy. Finally, the analysis presented takes into account a broad base of in-depth narrative interviews collected during several research projects on citizenship and civic participation with young Italians carried out over the last ten years (Colombo, 2010a, 2015; Colombo, Marchetti, & Domaneschi, 2011; Colombo & Rebughini, 2012).

ANALYSIS

The findings of the study are summarized in Table 6.1.

DEMOGRAPHIC/GENERAL CHARACTERISTICS

Eighty-seven females and 57 males (two people chose the 'other' option) took part in the survey. Half of them were aged between 18 and 20 years, a quarter of them were aged between 21 and 23 years and the remaining quarter were between 24 and 29 years old. Seventeen defined themselves as 'upper class', 109 as 'middle class' and 17 as 'working class'. Asked to freely indicate their cultural identification, the majority identified themselves on a national scale (88), 25 on a pan-national or cosmopolitan scale and 17 on regional or local basis. Thirteen chose multiple or hyphenated identifications for defining their cultural belonging. All of them identified Italian as their first language.

When asked to describe their personality type, 45 youngsters selected that of a friendly/relaxed/optimistic type, 31 chose a likes working alone/organized/introverted type, 28 chose a likes working with others/outgoing type and 23 selected a leader/driven to success/competitive type. Seventeen were a mix of personality types. Asked to indicate three main traits that summarized their own personality, the most recurrent terms were 'generous' (34), 'friendly' (30), 'organized' (23), 'outgoing' (22), 'competitive' (20) and 'optimistic' (20).

CITIZENSHIP EDUCATION AND INFORMATION

A large majority of respondents stated that they had studied civics in school, where they learned about government structures and processes. The civic notions learned, mainly during the classes of history or law, are considered important and useful (only three people said they were useless). However, 28 participants affirmed that citizenship education at

Table 6.1 Research findings with Italian youth

Italian youth	Number of participants: 146		
Demographics			
Gender	Male: 57	Female: 87	Other/Undisclosed: 2
Cultural identification	Italian		
First language	Italian		
	Yes	No	Do not remember
Citizenship education	88	47	11
	Knowledgeable	Some knowledge	Lack knowledge
Political knowledge	88	47	7
	Yes	No	Unsure
Follow the news	101	4	39
Personal political experience	34	101	9
Family's political involvement	103	25	16
Personality type	Assertive	Amiable Humanistic	Analytical
	23	45 28	31
	Important	Quite important	Not important
Attitude to community engagement	87	53	6
Attitude to political participation	96	24	1
	Effective	Somewhat effective	Ineffective
Level of personal efficacy	14	73	52
	Active	Somewhat active	Inactive
Civic involvement	35	79	29
	Supportive	Neutral	Do not care/not supportive
Attitudes towards democracy	100	23	4
Attitude towards govt. system in Italy	49	40	22
Students' civic participation (Top three)	Yes	No	No response
Being a good neighbour	131	8	7

(*continued*)

Table 6.1 (continued)

Italian youth	Number of participants: 146		
Helping those in need	131	10	5
Following political news	129	11	6
Granting Citizenship (Top three)	Important	Neutral	Not important	No response
To respect the law	129	4	1	2
To pay taxes	125	6	3	2
To be interested in the wellbeing of the community	112	17	4	3

school had been lacking and superficial, and that, due to its importance, it should be given more space and continuity.

Generally, Italian youngsters participating in our survey showed a consistent interest in being informed about social and political issues. Seven out of ten regularly followed the news, another quarter followed them sporadically and only four people said they were not interested at all in news. Young participants usually followed both national and international news. They were most interested in international news about wars and terrorism (97); social issues, both national (92) and local (89); global poverty (83); and environmental issues, both local (79) and global (79). A minority was interested in news about national politics (71), local transport (66) and the national economy (51). Even fewer were interested in news about national (45) and local (43) taxes or local new buildings projects (36).

Discussions with parents and friends are a privileged channel in the formation of political opinion and an important opportunity for information. The Internet is the main channel of information for young people surveyed: 109 say they acquire information online, 90 through watching TV and only 29 from reading newspapers. As other studies have shown (Cittalia, 2012), young people who use a mix of sources of information tend to be more informed and more active in the community: they are more likely to volunteer, join political parties and participate in protest. Young males who identify themselves as cosmopolitan are usually more interested in all kinds of information: local, national and global. Besides, they use the Internet more often and are more likely to participate in debate about social and political issues using social media. Young women are more interested than young men in international issues.

CIVIC PARTICIPATION

In the last years, a consistent number of studies have shown increasing disengagement from conventional political participation by western countries citizens, with young people playing a major role in distancing themselves from political involvement. Even in Italy, where participation in elections has been traditionally higher than in other European countries throughout the post-war period, research suggests that young people vote less, their membership in political parties is declining and their distrust of political institutions is rising (Istituto Giuseppe Toniolo, 2013). In 2012 (Istituto Nazionale di Statistica, ISTAT, 2013), only about 3.5 % of Italian young people aged between 19 and 34 years trusted national and local government, and trust was still lower for politicians and political parties. Even institutions that traditionally enjoyed broad trust by the majority of young Italians in recent years are seen with greater detachment. The percentage of young people who trust the police fell from 72 in 2004 to 45 in 2014; confidence in school and university dropped, in the same period, from 69 to 39; that of the Catholic Church from 52 to 32 (Buzzi, Cavalli, & De Lillo, 2007; Istituto Giuseppe Toniolo, 2014). This apparent form of youth detachment from political and civic participation can be interpreted as a reaction to frustrations young people are facing due to their increasingly difficult transitions to adult life. Integration into the labour market—one of the key tasks on a young person's way to autonomy—has become problematic, requiring high qualification, flexibility and willingness to navigate a long period of precariousness and insecurity. During the current Global Recession, integration into the labour market for young people has become all the more difficult and, since 2008, youth unemployment has increased substantially. High qualifications are no longer a guarantee for finding work, and access to the job market is not only difficult for young people who lack general or vocational education, but also for those holding higher education degrees (European Union Resolution 346 2012).[3] The youth unemployment rate is particularly high (44.2 % in 2014), and in the first three years after full-time education, less than half young people find a job; even if they find a job, it is often (64 %) temporary and considered, by 40 % of youngsters, to be disappointing and mismatched—in relation to salary and contents—with their educational level. The situation of the so-called NEET (not in employment, education or training) is particularly harsh. Although it is not a totally new phenomenon, the number of young NEET has grown rapidly since the beginning of the current economic and financial crisis: in 2013, in Italy, NEETs represented 33 % of 15–29 years old (ISTAT, 2014). The Italian media call them the 'lost generation', and they will certainly play a central social and political role in the future of the country.

Difficulties in employment and in imagining a way out of uncertainty and precariousness, as well as growing political corruption, help to explain young people's distrust of politicians and politics. They often perceive themselves as a generation crushed by older ones, who are in secure positions, do not intend to share their power positions with younger generations and are selfish, corrupted and unable to face the real problems of the country. As a result, young Italians tend to perceive politics as blocked by older generations and consider conventional political action an ineffective way to solve the problems of their precarious condition.

Our data confirm this picture but leave room for further observations. While the majority of our participants (87) think that it is important for people to be actively involved in improving their communities, only few of them (14) think that personal action can be effective to bring change to society. Young people who joined a political party are a minority (18), but the interest for politics is high. They consider themselves having good (15) or sufficient (73) knowledge of politics and government, and two out of five are regularly engaged in political activities such as talking about politics and getting involved in political activities. A large majority of them vote regularly (105) or occasionally (18); only 19 of them have never voted.

The feeling of being hindered or ignored by older generations often frustrates their interest and willingness to be active in civic process. Asked to explain how they consider themselves active in civic processes, some of them wrote:

> I would love to be more involved, I was, but I cannot hide to feel useless and never see any change. I notice however a serious lack of willingness to listen, to accept and welcome new people. (student #1)
>
> I am less active than I would like because it is useless and it does not change much, and frankly I would not even heard. (student #44)
>
> I feel that I could devote more time to civic initiatives but unfortunately often my schedule do not give me this opportunity; however, I do not think in today's society there are initiatives and space for young people, especially in the political sphere. (student #106)
>
> I wish there were more opportunities for young people's political action; but I do not see them. (student #126)

> Except with an occasional vote, I'm not involved in any way in the political activity. I think this is influenced by my little confidence in the current political world, and especially by the fact that politicians strongly influence any decision, often in a negative way and in fields that should not be influenced by political parties. (student #129)

However, our research indicates that young Italians have not disengaged from democratic and civic behaviour and that their democratic values are still strong. Only four participants did not care about democratic governance; two out of three considered democratic governance the best form of government. Asked to justify their opinion, some of them wrote:

> I support the democratic government for the freedom, rights and duties granted to citizens; maybe it is not perfect, but it is the best system of government we have. (student #30)
> The more I have to do with political life, the more I feel challenged. There are many contradictions and injustices in democracy. This does not lead me to reject it, but certain to be more careful and cautious in assessing its results. If you do not believe that democracy is the best form of government, you can observe its weaknesses and improve it. (student #74)
> Our grandparents fought for equality and democracy, and I would support them with all my strength. (student #120)

Rather than showing indifference and detachment from politics, young people are asking for more opportunities for participation and faster generational change. They want to have a say in public debates, and they expect those in power to listen to their opinions and take them seriously.

Participation in civic live is considered a way to self-fulfilment as well as a duty to society. Four out of five consider it important to participate in civic activities and contribute to the improvement of the well-being of the community.

In their words, participation is important because:

> Only with the participation, one can assert her own ideas. (student #43)
> Participate is a way to get involved and improve your own community. (student #35)
> We are citizens; we have the right and the duty to be concerned. (student #41)
> Participate is a way to be a driver of social change; to be a protagonist, not to delegate. (student #36)
> I believe that freedom is realized only through participation. (student #33)

Our participants do not exhibit a total rejection of politics; instead, they are interested in different forms of democratic activities appropriate to their own understanding of democracy and citizenship in a society in which they feel marginalized from the political process. Facing the distance and indifference of those in power, they are looking for new ways to make their voices heard.

Young Italians taking part in our survey have an active social life. Beside the traditional ways in which young people spend their leisure time—going out with friends, listening to music, watching TV, going to the cinema and attending music events, going shopping and going out for dinner—the majority of our participants are active users of social media (135) and play sports (103). One out of four is engaged in volunteering on regular basis. Considering people who are sometime engaged, the number of young people involved in volunteering rises to 65 %. By contrast, less than three out of ten participate in religious practices and, still less, in patriotic events.

Looking at the civic activities in which young respondents report they are engaged in, we can say that newer, more informal ways of participation are preferred (or, at least, add) to traditional ways of civic participation. Young people who defined themselves as active in the civic processes, leader, driven to succeed, competitive or a mix of personality types tend to adopt non-standard form of active civic participation such as boycotting, writing to newspapers and interacting and discussing issues on social media. Youngsters who define themselves as introverted and prefer solitary work tend to be less involved in civic activities. Political orientation plays a relevant role too. Young people who define themselves as close to the left part of the political spectrum tend to be more informed and active, especially in boycotts and protest.

Half of the Italian participants interact in discussions using social media; a significant number of them are involved in issue-based participation like signing petitions or spontaneously attending demonstrations, and consumer activism such as making shopping decisions based on political considerations. These non-standard forms of active civic participation are becoming part of the everyday landscape for a significant number—although not yet a majority—of young Italians. New technologies and online social communities, such as Facebook and Twitter, offer young people vast opportunities for personal politics and for mobilizing for political action across communities and borders.

Thirty-five (24.3 %) define themselves as active citizens, 79 as occasionally active and 29 as non-active (20.1 %). Self-defined active citizens tend to consider participation and engagement in social life an effective way to promote social change and to improve the well-being of the community; on the other hand, those who define themselves as non-active are more sceptical about the possibility to change society through personal actions.

The data collected show that a number of factors influence youth civic participation. As presented in Chap. 1, youth attitudes towards civic and political engagement can be advantageously understood as the dynamic outcome of the interaction between internal and contextual characteristics, as well as the ways in which concrete experiences are perceived, processed and evaluated. In general, we note that Italian girls tend to be more community-oriented. They are more likely to volunteer, getting involved in an issue and helping those in need. Boys are more often involved in writing to politicians, officials and newspapers. Self-descriptive identity has relevance too. Young people who define themselves as leaders and driven to succeed or using a mix of different personality traits are more likely to be civically and politically active, while young people who describe themselves as introverted and preferring to work alone are less likely to be involved in civic or political actions. Cosmopolitan outlook seems to play a relevant role in promoting youth participation; young people who depict themselves as not strongly tied to just one belonging are more likely to join a political party, protest, boycott and donate money to causes. Contextual factors such as family and school also have impact on civic engagement. In general, Italian young people from families in which parents are politically active tend to be more engaged and informed. Young people who studied civic education at school and learned about government structure and processes are likely to be more involved in civic and political activities.

THE COMPLEXITY OF BELONGING

Young people born at the end of the last century share specific social experiences—that can be summarized under the label 'globalization'—that place them in a potentially new social location (Anthias, 2013). Technological improvements in communication and transport favour the global circulations of ideas, images, imaginaries, goods and people that have modified the concept of local, belonging and engagement. In a new way when compared to the past, facts, news and commodities that originate in places far away from their context of daily life increasingly affect young people's lives. Feeling part of a community is no longer necessarily tied to sharing the same geographical territory: people and facts geographically distant can be perceived as affecting personal life and requiring personal involvement more than people or fact that happen in the neighbourhood, or next-door (Harris, 2013; Kallio, Häkli, & Bäcklund, 2015).

The feeling of being part of a community and the drive to contribute to its improvement emerge as the product of the ongoing process of 'manoeuvring' between individual personality, global flux of ideas, information and networks in which people are embedded, structural aspects of the social contexts in which young people act and the way they deal practically with these contexts, their resources and their constraints (Colombo & Rebughini, 2012). Belonging becomes a matter of 'choice', and multiple belonging becomes a way to manage levels of participation and engagement in different contexts in order to better realize personal goals, while at the same time reducing the risks of personal losses.

In this scenario, the idea of civic engagement and active citizenship (cfr. Chap. 1) changes. Feeling part of a community and being recognized as a citizen is no longer necessarily tied to ascribed factors such as being born in a specific place or community. Instead, it becomes something that is connected with subjective characteristics, choices, values and behaviours. Being part of the same community does not mean being 'similar', the possibility to freely display individual preferences and diversity is considered an essential facet of full citizenship (Isin & Turner, 2010).

Our participants support this vision of citizenship. Asked to describe what personal characteristics, norms, values, and behaviours are appropriate for those claiming membership in a political community, the majority of respondents use words such 'participation' (27), 'being informed' (23), 'respect of rules and law' (23) and 'honesty' (16).

Figure 6.1 summarizes the portrait of a good citizen resulting from our survey responses. What should characterize good citizens is their respect for rules and law, especially when it comes to paying taxes, and their interest in the well-being of the community, getting involved and acting as good neighbours. The knowledge of the majority language and of the history and institution of the country, as well having a regular job, are deemed to be other important aspects for being a good citizen. On the other hand, young people interviewed do not think that strong sameness is a relevant requirement for citizenship entitlement. People and groups following different religions or lifestyles ought to be recognized

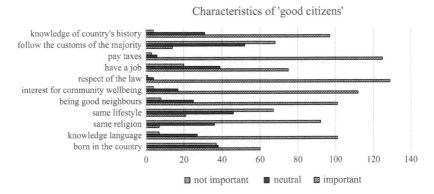

Fig. 6.1 Characteristics of good citizens (number of respondents)

as members of the community if they are involved in it and show interest for its improvement. Rather than based on sameness, citizenship is the space where differences are accepted and respected, where people are recognized as free to express their own preferences and interests, with the only constraint being to respect the preferences and interest of other members of the community. Citizenship has to do with the recognition of individual freedom and has to assure equal opportunity; it involves behavioural and attitudinal aspects rather than innate characteristics (Benedicto & Morán, 2007; Passini, 2014). Young people put emphasis on the participative dimensions of citizenship, while ascribed dimensions (determined by fate or blood or individual choices regarding the intimate preferences) remain in the background.

It is relevant to underline that, despite the historical relevance that religion has played and continues to play in the Italian society, young people do not consider professing the same faith a fundamental characteristic of being entitled to citizenship.

In general, the idea of citizenship that results from our data highlights an important generation shift. While, historically, Italian citizenship has been seen as a 'primordial' and ascribed characteristic, connected with kinship and 'blood', young people answering our survey conceive it as related to proper behaviours and individual characteristics.

This new attitude is fostered by specific generational experiences. In fact, only since the eighties of the last century has Italy become a country of immigration, and our participants represent the first generation growing up in a truly multicultural context, developing a different attitude towards cultural diversity.

Migration in Italy has become a structural dimension. In the last 30 years, Italian schools have become more culturally complex; children of immigrant backgrounds currently represent about 10 % of the pupils, but are more than 20 % of the total in the most affluent parts of the country. Children of immigrants in Italian schools have very different family backgrounds. Their parents came from a large spectrum of countries, and no immigrant community counts for more than 20 % of the total. As a result, classrooms are often really multicultural, and the issue of living together with difference is central for both teachers and pupils. The experience of children with different ethno-cultural familiar backgrounds, growing up together in the same environment, poses new questions about the meaning of nationhood, belonging and citizenship. The issue becomes particularly problematic when the incongruences of the current Italian citizenship law are taken into account. Half of the children of immigrants attending Italian schools are born in Italy but do not have Italian citizenship, due to the *jus sanguinis* principle of the current law. Children of foreign parents who are born in Italy are not automatically recognized as Italian, let alone entitled to stay in the country. On the contrary, they need to fulfil a series of tricky requirements in order to apply for Italian citizenship. In fact, they have just one year to submit their application (they must be between 18 and 19); they must prove they have been living in Italy without interruption; moreover, their parents have to have been legally recognized at the moment of the child's birth and to have remained so for the entire period until the coming of age of the son or the daughter. This latter requirement is particularly penalizing for the children who end up paying for the 'faults' of their parents. Around half of the foreigners who currently hold a regular permit to stay have previous experiences of irregular migration. Moreover, it is quite common for parents to decide to raise their children in the country of origin, at least for a short period of time, due to the long hours and harsh working conditions in Italy that do not allow them to take care of their children adequately, or because, by entrusting their children to relatives in their country of origin, they want their kids to learn their native language and traditions. Although they were born in Italy and spent much of their life there, children of immigrants who fail to obtain Italian citizenship when they come of age have to apply for a regular permit to stay, without which they may be expelled from Italy, to the country of their parents that they barely know and are not interested in living in.

Public discussion about the necessity for a new citizenship law has been quite intense in the last years, as well as a strong centre of political activity for a significant number of children of immigrants (see for instance the website of one of the most important second-generation youth association at www.secondegenerazioni.it).

Italian young people—also due to their experience of pluralistic and multicultural schools—seem to support a radical revision of the principles of Italian citizenship, overcoming a strict *ius sanguinis* rule, in favour of a more tolerant *ius soli* rule. Our participants, further, show a polarized attitude towards the recognition and acceptance of cultural diversity. On the one hand, young people with higher cultural capital, who locate themselves on the left or centre-left of the political spectrum and auto-describe as leader, driven to succeed and competitive, tend to give less importance to ethnic background and consider citizenship as strictly connected with individual characteristics. For most of them, anyone who contributes to the well-being of society, works, obeys the law, pay taxes, is economically self-reliant and is tolerant towards others' difference can and actually should have citizenship. Nevertheless, the emphasis on participation, independence and self-governance is not devoid from potential problematic aspects. The idea that citizenship constitutes a guarantee of entitlement of equal rights, regardless of actual personal behaviour, does not seem to be very widespread. Instead, citizenship is perceived as a 'reward' for those who behave properly and contribute to the idea that it is possible to differentiate between series A persons (the 'good citizens', the 'right ones', the 'followers of the rules') and series B persons (the 'marginal', the 'deviants', the 'bad' or 'non-citizens') (Colombo, 2010b; Lister, Smith, Middleton, & Cox, 2003). The former must be guaranteed and protected while the latter must be left to their fate and excluded from citizenship rights. The universalistic and inclusive principles that have oriented the development of citizenship in western countries during modernity—in the effort to broaden inclusion and participation in public life as much as possible and to reduce economic and social divisions—is replaced by a criterion of merit that converts rights into rewards that must be earned through active and compliant behaviour (Colombo, 2015; Ong, 2006).

On the other hand, young people who participate less in civic and political life, who locate themselves on the right of the political spectrum and auto-describe as introverted, organized and preferring to work alone tend to be more hostile towards cultural diversity. They reproduce the well-known rhetoric of the so-called symbolic (Sears, 1988) and covert (Coates, 2011) racism. Migrants are perceived as a cultural threat and blamed for the excessive attention the state pays to them, which undermines the principle of equality and justice.

A focus group participant, attending a vocational school, sympathizer of a populist right party and from a working class family, expressed this kind of position well:

> We are discriminated, foreigners have more rights ... they can do what they want, they commit crimes, push drugs, squat in public housing when Italian poor people are left without any help ... I'm not racism, but they forced me to be so ... when I see that they have all the support and we are left alone, I think that we are discriminated ... a right politics would put Italian people first. I'm ok with foreigners that come here and respect our rules, but they cannot be treated differently from Italians, if they commit crimes they have to be expelled ... no justification! No tolerance! (Focus group 1, student C)

A NEW GENERATION OF CITIZENS

The image of young citizens emerging from the Italian part of this research is complex. While it confirms that Italian youngsters demonstrate a strong detachment from political engagement and express severe criticisms towards the generation in power, it also highlights that they are interested in civic participation, are well informed about their rights and duties, know the main rules and functioning of institutions and value democracy as an effective way to promote equality, justice and individual and collective well-being.

What is evident is that their willingness to participate is frustrated by not being taken seriously by older generations. These are blamed for occupying privileged positions in politics and economics and for defending their advantages without taking into account the needs and interests of younger generations. Politicians, and adults in general, are accused of being selfish, interested only in taking personal advantages and defending their own interests. Disengagement in politics and in classical forms of civic participation is mainly due to the perception of their uselessness, the idea that young people's voice is not heard and not taken seriously. Therefore, a significant number among them look for other, non-standard, forms of civic engagement, such as boycotting, buycotting or interacting in activities, discussions and protests using social media. Rather than a radical decline of interest in politics, we are witnessing a decline in political capital (Tonge, Mycock, & Jeffery, 2012), that is, citizens' trust in and respect for the institutions of the political system and canonical forms of politic actions such as voting, join a political party and campaign activism. Young people interested in politics are looking for new ways of effective participation, new forms of action affecting the society and promoting real changes.

New forms of civic participation are made possible by improvements in communication technology and by growing global interconnections. Young people are a generation growing up familiar with social media, cultural difference and the capacity/necessity to manage more languages and codes to face the different and changeable contexts in which they act. The complexity, variability and unpredictability of the different situations in which they are involved, situations that require flexibility and adequateness, call for new generational skills that privilege the capacity to fit the contest rather than showing a coherence that quickly transforms itself into a burden that hinders the reaching of personal goals. Educators and schools should pay more attention to innovative forms of civic engagement and orient new generational skills to their use for the good of the community. Civic education should give more attention to 'practical' engagement and less to teaching institutional, formal rules.

It is important to highlight that the development of these new generational skills depends on personal capacity (Melucci, 1996), that is, all those resources available to an individual to think of herself and act as an individual, to be recognized as such by others and to invest in self-realization as human being. The capacity/possibility to develop an adequate personal capacity relies on individual, familiar, social and structural resources that are unequally distributed. In order to be active citizens in a globalized world, it is no longer sufficient to be 'trained' in the rule of society and its government. People have to learn to select appropriate information, to understand which rules are suitable, which behaviours are viable and which objectives are realistic for the specific situation in which they act. Participation in social life requires more information, more capacity to understand differences and to accept, or at least tolerate, them; young people have to be able to create new forms of action fitting the specific characteristics of the situation, to learn different languages and codes to be able to communicate, to express their preferences and defend their interests.

Consequences for an Effective Citizenship Education

The specific social location of this young generation necessitates more, and more effective, citizenship education that should be able to take into account new forms of involvement and to stimulate new forms of action that support active citizenship (Broom, 2010). Beside 'training' about rules and laws, the functioning of democratic institutions and the values that underpin them, a contemporary education about citizenship should be open to innovative forms of participation, stimulating direct and active experiences in different contexts, for different communities, responsive to different forms of belonging. Living in a democratic global society requires citizens to be able to manage different codes, be open to social and cultural difference, be competent in debating social issues and be keen to make their contribution to the improvement of the community.

Rather than being apathetic and disengaged, significant numbers of young people ask to be taken seriously and aspire to have their voices heard and to have a say in collective issues. They want to be protagonists of their future and active in social change. Citizenship education represents a needed tool for preparing new generations to become active citizens, but it requires being attentive to individual personality, the specificity of the local environment and the constraints and resources available at the macro level. Educators should involve young people more in practical actions, oriented to produce tangible improvement in the daily environment of youth life. Moral education, that is, helping young people acquire moral habits that help them to become active and contributing members of their community, can no longer be excluded from school curricula and left to the sole task of families. Moral and civic education, so long separated in the Italian tradition of education, should find a new synthesis that places at its core active learning and the direct experience of young people.

A complex, global democratic society requires new form of civic engagement and participation, aiming at enlarging inclusion and stimulating personal capacity; young people are a resource indispensable to a democratic society that seeks to effectively address the challenges of a complex and multicultural society. It is up to older generation to be able to leave adequate room for young people to participate in the building of our future society.

Notes

1. https://wcd.coe.int/ViewDoc.jsp?id=1621697.
2. High schools in Italy comprise three different types: Lyceum, Technical Institute and Professional Institute.
3. https://wcd.coe.int/ViewDoc.jsp?id=1991759&Site=COE.

References

Ainley, J., Friedman, T., Kerr, D., & Schulz, W. (2012, September 18). *Assessing the intended participation of young adolescents as future citizens: Comparing results from 26 European countries.* Paper presented at European Conference on Educational Research, Cádiz, Spain.

Anthias, F. (2013). Hierarchies of social location, class and intersectionality: Towards a translocational frame. *International Sociology, 28*(1), 121–138. doi:10.1177/0268580912463155.

Arthur, J., & Davies, I. (Eds.) (2008). *Citizenship education.* London: Sage.

Bauman, Z. (1995). *Life in fragments.* Oxford: Blackwell.

Beaumont, E. (2010). Political agency and empowerment: Pathways for developing a sense of political efficacy in young adults. In L. R. Sherrod, J. Torney-Purta, & C. A. Flanagan (Eds.), *Handbook of research on civic engagement in youth* (pp. 525–668). Hoboken, NJ: John Wiley & Sons.

Beck, U. (1992). *Risk society: Towards a new modernity.* London: Sage.

Benedicto, J., & Morán, M. L. (2007). Becoming a citizen. *European Society, 9*(4), 601–622. doi:10.1080/14616690701314085.

Bennet, L. W. (2007). Civic learning in changing democracies: Challenges for citizenship and civic education. In P. Dahlgren (Ed.), *Young citizens and new media: Learning democratic engagement* (pp. 59–78). New York: Routledge.

Broom, C. (2010). Conceptualizing and teaching citizenship as humanity. *Citizenship, Social and Economics Education, 9*(3), 147–155. doi:10.2304/csee.2010.9.3.147.

Buzzi, C., Cavalli, A., & de Lillo, A. (2007). *Rapporto giovani. Sesta indagine dell'Istituto IARD sulla condizione giovanile in Italia.* Bologna: Il Mulino.

Cavalli, A., & Deiana, G. (1999). *Educare alla cittadinanza democratica.* Milano: Franco Angeli.

Coates, R. D. (Ed.) (2011). *Covert racism.* Boston: Brill.

Colombo, E. (2010a). Crossing differences: How young children of immigrants keep everyday multiculturalism alive. *Journal of Intercultural Studies, 31*(5), 455–470. doi:10.1080/07256868.2010.513081.

Colombo, E. (2010b). Changing citizenship: Everyday representations of membership, belonging and identification among Italian senior secondary school students. *Italian Journal of Sociology of Education*, *4*(1), 129–153. doi:10.14658/pupj-ijse-2010-1-6.

Colombo, E. (2015). Complicating citizenship. How children of immigrants in Italy represent belonging and rights. In R. Marback (Ed.), *Generations. Rethinking age and citizenship* (pp. 134–156). Detroit: Wayne State University Press.

Colombo, E., Domaneschi, L., & Marchetti, C. (2011). Citizenship and multiple belonging. Representations of inclusion, identification and participation among children of immigrants in Italy. *Journal of Modern Italian Studies, 16*(3), 334–347. doi:10.1080/1354571X.2011.565630.

Colombo, E., & Rebughini, P. (2012). *2012 Children of immigrants in a globalized world. A generational experience*. Basingstoke: Palgrave Macmillan.

EACEA Eurydice (2012). *Citizenship education in Europe*. Brussels: Education, Audiovisual and Culture Executive Agency. doi:10.2797/83012.

Harris, A. (2013). *Young people and everyday multiculturalism*. New York: Routledge.

Harris, A., Wyn, J., & Youness, S. (2010). Beyond apathetic or activist youth: 'Ordinary' young people and contemporary forms of participation. *Young (Nordic Journal of Youth Research), 18*(1), 9–32. doi:10.1177/110330880901800103.

Isin, E. F., & Turner, B. S. (2010). Citizenship, cosmopolitanism and human rights. In A. Elliott (Ed.), *The Routledge companion to social theory* (pp. 173–187). Milton Park: Routledge.

ISTAT (2013). *Rapporto BES 2013: Il benessere equo e sostenibile in Italia*. Roma: ISTAT. http://www.istat.it/it/archivio/84348

ISTAT (2014). *Rapporto annuale 2014. La situazione del Paese*. Roma: ISTAT. www.istat.it/it/files/2014/05/Rapporto-annuale-2014.pdf

Istituto Giuseppe Toniolo (2013). *La condizione giovanile in Italia. Rapporto giovani 2013*. Bologna: Il Mulino.

Istituto Giuseppe Toniolo (2014). *La condizione giovanile in Italia. Rapporto giovani 2014*. Bologna: Il Mulino.

Jowell, R., & Park, A. (1998). *Young people, politics and citizenship: A disengaged generation?* London, UK: Citizenship Foundation.

Kallio, K. P., Häkli, J., & Bäcklund, P. (2015). Lived citizenship as the locus of political agency in participatory policy. *Citizenship Studies, 19*(1), 101–119. doi:10.1080/13621025.2014.982447.

Kimberlee, R. (1998). Politically apathetic youth: A new generation? *Renewal, 6*(2), 87–90.

Levine, P. (2007). *The future of democracy: Developing the next generation of American citizens*. Medford, MA/Hanover: Tufts University Press.

Lister, R., Smith, N., Middleton, S., & Cox, L. (2003). Young people talk about citizenship: Empirical perspectives on theoretical and political debate. *Citizenship Studies, 7*(2), 235–253. doi:10.1080/1362102032000065991.

Macedo, S., Alex-Assenhoh, Y., & Berry, J. (2005). *Democracy at risk: How political choices undermine citizen participation, and what we can do about it.* Washington, DC: Brooks Institution Press.

Means, A.J. (2015). Generational precarity, education, and the crisis of capitalism: Conventional, neo-Keynesian, and Marxian perspectives. *Critical Sociology,* publ. on-line January 8, 2015. 0896920514564088

Melo, D. F., & Stockemer, D. (2014). Age and political participation in Germany, France and the UK: A comparative analysis. *Comparative European Politics,* *12*(1), 33–53. doi:10.1057/cep.2012.31.

Melucci, A. (1996). *Challenging codes.* Cambridge: Cambridge University Press.

Ong, A. (2006). Mutations in citizenship. *Theory, Culture & Society,* *23*(2–3), 499–505. doi:10.1177/0263276406064831.

Passini, S. (2014). Adolescent's common sense understanding of rights and duties: The effect of the individualization of rights on a rights dilemma. *Youth & Society,* *46*(4), 460–477. doi:10.1177/0044118X12438905.

Putnam, R. (2000). *Bowling alone: The collapse and revival of American community.* New York: Touchstone.

Schulz, W., Ainley, J., Fraillon, J., Kerr, D., & Losito, B. (2010). *ICCS 2009 International report: Civic knowledge, attitudes, and engagement among lower secondary school students in 38 countries.* Amsterdam: International Association for the Evaluation of Educational Achievement (IEA).

Sears, D. O. (1988). Symbolic racism. In P. A. Katz & D. A. Taylor (Eds.), *Eliminating racism: Profiles in controversy* (pp. 53–84). New York: Plenum Press.

Sloam, J. (2014). 'The outraged young': Young Europeans, civic engagement and the new media in a time of crisis. *Information, Communication & Society,* *17*(2), 217–231. doi:10.1080/1369118X.2013.868019.

Tonge, J., Mycock, J., & Jeffery, B. (2012). Does citizenship education make young people better-engaged citizens? *Political Studies,* *60*(3), 578–602. doi:10.1111/j.1467-9248.2011.00931.x.

Zaff, J. F., Boyd, M., Li, Y., Lerner, J. V., & Lerner, R. M. (2010). Active and engaged citizenship: Multi-group and longitudinal factorial analysis of an integrated construct of civic engagement. *Journal of Youth Adolescence,* *39*, 736–750. doi:10.1007/s10964-010-9541-6.

Zukin, C., Keeter, S., Andolina, M., Jenkins, K., & Delli Carpini, M. X. (2006). *A new engagement? Political participation, civic life and the changing American citizen.* Oxford: Oxford University Press.

CHAPTER 7

Citizenship Education in Japan: Past, Present, and Future

Keiichi Takaya

As I write this chapter in the Fall of 2015, things are changing rather dramatically. We have recently witnessed two incidents that may raise Japanese youth's social awareness and involvement. First, the Diet passed a bill that lowered the voting age from 20 to 18 in June 2015; youth as young as 12th grade will start going to the polls. Second, from August to September this year, many people including students took to the streets—this is something unusual in Japan at least in the past 30 years—protesting Prime Minister Shinzo Abe's "re-interpretation" of the pacifist provision of the Constitution and the passage of bills that would allow Self-Defense Forces to be deployed overseas. I hope that these incidents will lead to youth's greater engagement, but the prospect is uncertain at this point of time.

If the purpose of citizenship education is not limited to providing students with basic knowledge about their society but also includes encouraging them to understand and participate in civic processes, Japanese schools are not doing it adequately. My purpose in this chapter is to point out where Japanese schools fail in this regard and to suggest how we may address these problems.

K. Takaya (✉)
Faculty of Letters, Kokugakuin University, Tokyo, Japan
e-mail: keiichi_takaya@yahoo.co.jp

© The Author(s) 2017
C. Broom (ed.), *Youth Civic Engagement in a Globalized World*,
Palgrave Studies in Global Citizenship Education and Democracy,
DOI 10.1057/978-1-137-56533-4_7

WHAT IS CITIZENSHIP EDUCATION?

Citizenship education, in terms of its content, may mean two types of education (see also Chap. 1). It can, and sometimes actually does, mean the same thing as socialization or even indoctrination; in this sense, its main objective is to develop appropriate attitudes, values, knowledge and skills that are conducive to maintaining a nation (I will call this type of education 1-A). Citizenship education can also mean the acquisition of objective knowledge, conceptual tools, and analytic skills that are necessary to understand the characteristics of one's own society as well as various other societies. In this latter sense, citizenship education may include the cultivation of perspectives and values that transcend those of one's own society (1-B).

When we look at the curriculum and teaching methods, citizenship education can be conducted in two ways. First, it can be the end of public education as a whole; from this perspective, we must examine the whole structure of public education if we want to examine the scope of citizenship education in a nation (2-A). Second, it can be dealt with in a subject or a group of subjects: usually, the area known as social studies or its subdisciplines such as civics and history (2-B).

In Japan, citizenship education in terms of 1-B and 2-B is relatively new. The subjects which deal with citizenship education, such as Social Studies (*Shakai*), Politics and Economy (*Seiji keizai*), and Civics (*Koumin*), were introduced only after the Second World War. On the other hand, citizenship education in terms of 1-A has not only existed from the very beginning of Japan's modern educational system but has also been the central concern of it. It is, however, not so easy to sort out where and how it was done.

The overwhelming focus of citizenship education since the establishment of the modern school system in the late 19th century to the end of the Second World War was the inculcation of patriotism. This aim was clearly stated in various official orders and documents, and students were frequently made to understand that the end of their education was to become loyal subjects of the emperor through not only lessons but also extra-curricular activities and ceremonies (Yamazumi, 1997, 2007). A few subjects were especially designated to deal with this part of education: Moral Education or Self-government (*Shushin*), Geography (*Chiri*), and National History (*Kokushi*). As the scope of citizenship education varies depending on how you define it, we may have to look at some other subject areas and activities than the ones I just mentioned; for example, many reading materials in the textbooks for Japanese (*Kokugo*) contained patriotic themes.

Subjects that deal with citizenship education become important, usually, at the secondary level. In Japan, as well as in other nations, however, very few students went on to secondary schools before the Second World War. An overwhelming majority of students, if they had a chance to receive any post-primary schooling, received vocational education, and in such schools, academic understanding of society (1-B) was considered irrelevant or even miseducative.

There were a few exceptions; what some regard as precursors of postwar social studies existed in some of these vocational schools, for example, subjects called Law and Economics (*Housei oyobi keizai*) and Civics (*Koumin*). They were, however, exceptions and very few, less than 10 % of the same age-group at most, received them (Matsuno, 1997).

New Directions for Citizenship Education: Learning from the Past and Learning from Overseas

Educators today regard citizenship education as a crucial part of educating youth for the globalizing world. In Japan, publications on the topic are on the rise (e.g. Kodama, 2010; Nakayama et al., 2010; Ikeno, 2011). For those Japanese educators who are concerned with citizenship education, an important theoretical source is Bernard Crick's work (particularly the Crick Report [the Advisory Group on Citizenship, 1998]), but they draw on other sources as well (e.g. UNESCO, 1998; see also, Nakayama et al., 2010, p. 1; Fujiwara, 2011).

Japan is not without educational traditions that at least somewhat dealt with 1-B. *Tsuzuri-kata* (spelling and composition), for example, was a branch or a type of Japanese instruction, which spread relatively widely and had significant impact. It was quite exceptional and unique because some teachers who adopted the approach even encouraged students to choose their own topics, explore them thoroughly, and freely express their own thoughts and feelings while assisting them with improving structures and expressions of their writings (e.g. Muchaku, 1953; Kokubun, 1955; Tsurumi, 1995; Yamazumi, 1995). *Tsuzuri-kata* may be comparable to Paulo Freire's (1970) approach to teaching literacy to the oppressed because students, particularly in impoverished areas, came to understand social ills and injustices through writing on their personal experiences.

EDUCATIONAL REFORM AFTER THE SECOND WORLD WAR

US-led Allied Forces occupied Japan after the Second World War and tried to eradicate the sources of Japan's expansionism and militarism (1945–52). As part of their attempts to democratize and demilitarize Japanese society, America sent an education mission to Japan in March 1946. They cooperated with a committee of Japanese educators and submitted *The Report of the US Education Mission to Japan* (1946) to the General Headquarters of the Occupation Forces. The Japanese Ministry of Education eventually accepted the recommendations.

In the new system, secondary schools (the junior high school, grades 7–9, and the senior high school, grades 10–12) became mostly single-track. Experience-based education, inspired most notably by John Dewey, became popular and in some cases replaced lecturing and drilling. The new social studies courses (1-B) were considered particularly amenable to the experience-based method.

Unfortunately, Japanese education—its administrative organization, curriculum, and teaching methods—took a reverse turn to some degree in the 1950s due to such political and economic factors as the Cold War and economic growth. Industries' demand for the efficient training of a high-quality work force were matched by the needs of students and their parents who came to regard education largely as a pragmatic means for personal well-being and social promotion (Horio, 1995). For them, what mattered was a fair and objective assessment of academic achievements in exams at various points, and for that purpose, traditional methods and content that emphasized standardized factual knowledge suited well. However, some lessons related to citizenship education tried to raise children's environmental awareness. From the 1950s through the early 1970s when Japan's economy rapidly expanded, severe incidents of air, water, and soil pollution happened and many people suffered from them. The problems were so widespread and serious that social studies textbooks and lessons just could not avoid them in teaching about Japanese society (e.g. Ishikawa, 2010).

SOME OBSERVATIONS ON THE CURRENT STATE OF CITIZENSHIP EDUCATION IN JAPAN

Rohlen (1983), Lewis (1995), and Benjamin (1997) observe that while Japanese elementary education is full of child-centered, creative activities, junior and senior high schools neglect the joy of learning and focus almost exclusively on the acquisition of content knowledge under the pressure of preparing students for entrance exams.

Although competition has eased significantly in the past 20 years due to the decreasing number of children, the overall pattern of education has not changed. This is partly due to what society expects of young people in their late teens in Japan. Japanese tend to think that social understandings come only with maturation and with real-life experience after graduation (Rohlen, 1983), which excuses schools from dealing with real-life issues. Thus, basic knowledge is emphasized while students' engagement is paid only lip-service. Rohlen (1983) finds it ironic that even such themes as individual freedom and civic participation are lectured in Japanese high schools.

The aims and contents of social studies courses look promising. In junior high school, Social Studies (*shakai*) is a required subject in all grades and includes geography, Japanese history, and civics; the major goals of its civics-related part (usually taught in 9th grade) are to understand democracy and to acquire relevant knowledge for civic participation. The topics include, for example, how decisions are made and conflicts are resolved in our society (in family, school and workplace, and local community), the mechanisms of the market economy, how democratic processes work and the significance of civic participation, and the role of local and national governments in promoting welfare and well-being (The Ministry of Education, Culture, Sports, Science and Technology, 2008). In senior high schools, students are required to take at least a year of either Contemporary Society (*Gendai shakai*), Ethics (*Rinri*), or Politics and Economy (*Seiji keizai*). These subjects' scopes and topics are not very different from those of junior high schools' social studies, but have greater width and depth.

The problem, however, is that the curriculum and textbooks try to introduce as many topics as possible within limited numbers of pages. Consequently, teachers have barely enough time to skim through the topics, and virtually no time for classroom discussion or individual inquiry and exploration. The emphasis on knowledge by itself may not be the heart of the problem, since knowledge is important in any field. What I find problematic about this approach is that, as I will show later when I discuss research findings, factual knowledge does not seem to stick in students' minds with the kinds of curriculum and teaching methods used; many Japanese students seem to be finding social studies useless, irrelevant, or uninteresting because it does not deal with facts and concepts in a way that would allow them to realize the relevance of such knowledge in understanding how society works and what part they may be able to play.

Research Findings on Youth Engagement

I conducted a study that consisted of questionnaires and interviews on Japanese youth's social and political awareness and involvement. Like the other researchers, I used SPSS descriptive statistical analysis (cross-tabs). The study was conducted in the Fall of 2014, that is, before the political events described at the beginning of this chapter.

Since the participants were limited in number and may not have been well-distributed across socio-economic or cultural strata, I do not claim that my findings have much statistical significance. The participants, however, are not atypical of today's Japanese youth and I think my findings can show you some characteristics of Japanese youth today. Also, I think that what my findings can show will be, if anything at all, hypotheses on which more research may be designed.

I conducted the survey at the university where I teach, which is a middle-sized private university in Tokyo.[1] The student population of the university is about 10,000, including a small number of graduate students. The university does not have natural science majors and is not particularly prestigious or academically top-rated, but it has very strong programs in Japanese history and literature (it grants doctorates in these areas). One thing that makes our university unique is that it has a Shinto major, which trains Shinto priests (only two universities in Japan have such a program). The university's student population, however, is not predominantly religious, partly because the Shinto program is small and Japanese society in general is not very religious.

In Japan, about 55 % of youth pursue higher education today.[2] Public universities are more prestigious and have better facilities and smaller student–teacher ratios, although there are a few private universities that have equally good or even better reputations than some public universities.

DEMOGRAPHICS AND GENERAL CHARACTERISTICS

A total of 177 students (74 males and 103 females) participated in the survey and most of them were between the ages of 18 and 21 (161 = about 91 %; only one student was over 25) (Table 7.1).

The students were in varied programs from Literature to Law, Economics, and Shinto, and no international students were among them (the university has only a handful of international students; barely 1 % of the total number of students[3]).

Table 7.1 Japan's summary of findings

Japanese youth	*Number of participants: 177*			
Demographics				
Gender	Male: 74	Female: 103	Other/Undisclosed: 0	
Cultural identification	Japanese: 50	Other: 11	Do not know/Missing: 41	
First language	Japanese: 177	Other: 0		
	Yes	No	Do not remember	
Citizenship education	155	10	12	
	Knowledgeable	Some knowledge	Lack knowledge	
Political knowledge	n/a	n/a	n/a	
	Yes	No	Unsure	
Follow the news	79	77	n/a	
Personal political experience	30	101	Do not remember: 44	
Family's political involvement	50	36	Do not know: 89	
Personality type	Assertive/Competitive	Amiable/Spontaneous	Humanistic/Expressive	Analytical/Methodical
	9	41	40	42
	Important	Somewhat important	Not very important/Does not matter	
Attitude to community engagement	n/a	n/a	n/a	
Attitude to political participation	68	59	11	
	Effective	Somewhat effective	Ineffective	
Level of personal efficacy	n/a	n/a	n/a	
	Active	Somewhat active/occasionally active	Not very active/Not active or interested	
Civic involvement	2	57	105	
	Very interested/somewhat interested	Cannot tell	Not very interested/Not interested	
Attitudes toward democracy	110	26	37	
Attitude toward govt. system in Japan	28	82	39	

(*continued*)

Table 7.1 (continued)

Japanese youth	Number of participants: 177		
Students' civic participation (Top 3)	Yes	No	No response
News following	88	89	0
Voting	36	141	0
Volunteering	33	144	0
Granting Citizenship (Top 3)	n/a	n/a	n/a
To know the language			
To know history and laws			
To be a good neighbor			
Correlations			
Internal			
Personality-voting	Significant correlation, X^2 (4, N = 133) = 12.418, p = .014		
Personality-volunteering	No significant correlation		
Personality-participation	No significant correlation		
External:			
Education-participation	$X2$ (10, N = 177) = 18.330, p = .050		
Active family-participation	Significant correlation, X^2 (10, N = 175) = 16.233, p = .093		
Political experience-participation	Significant correlation, X^2 (10, N = 175) = 24.851, p =.006		
Culture-participation	X^2 (10, N = 102) = 17.238, p = .069		

As I wrote above, everyone is supposed to have studied about citizenship in such subjects as Social Studies, Contemporary Society, or Politics and Economy because they are required subjects in junior and senior high schools. Ten students, however, replied that they had not taken such subjects (it is highly unlikely that they had actually not) and 12 replied that they did not remember.

Even though our university is a Shinto university, only 19 students (10.7 %) answered that they had a religious faith, mostly either Shinto or Buddhism. This is actually lower than the national average. According to the polls conducted by the NHK Broadcasting (2015), among youth between the ages of 16 and 29, 16 % believed in *hotoke* (Buddhist deities) and 21 % believed in *kami* (this term is somewhat ambiguous; it could mean either Shinto deities or Christian/Jewish/Islamic God) (p. 136).

Social Class and Cultural/Ethnic Backgrounds

The students' replies regarding their social class and cultural/ethnic backgrounds were, in a sense, very interesting. Three students (1.7 %) replied as "upper middle class", 80 (45.2 %) as "middle class", and 16 (9.0 %) as "working class". Twelve students (6.8 %) replied "Don't know" and 45 (25.4 %) wrote something else, such as "student".

As to cultural and ethnic identity, 50 students (28.2 %) wrote either Japan or Japanese (all of them were supposed to be Japanese since there were no international students among the participants). Eleven (6.2 %) wrote something else, but none of them indicated any ethnicity or cultural tradition. Forty-one (23.2 %) replied "Don't know" and 75 (42.4 %) did not reply.

When I conducted the survey, I asked the participants to write "Don't know" or to so indicate, rather than leave it blank, if the question did not make sense to them. So I gather that the questions about social class and culture/ethnicity did not make sense to many of them. It is odd that many students were not familiar with these issues and concepts as social class because such issues as race, ethnicity, religious and cultural diversity, and economic discrepancy are among the issues that must be covered in high school social studies courses according to the *National Course of Study*.

The National Course of Study, in the section on junior high school social studies, mandates that such topics as gender equality, social tolerance, and the reduction of poverty be covered (The Ministry of Education, Culture, Sports, Science and Technology, 2008). Although it also recommends the use of presentation, discussion, and essay, only the coverage of the topics seems to be done in most of the cases. A problem might be that the *Course of Study* tends to emphasize a "balanced" approach, meaning that teachers are expected to avoid emphasizing a specific perspective or a specific part of a topic and to give an even-handed overview of the topics. This makes it hard for teachers to encourage their students to inquire into specific topics in depth or to develop their own ideas and arguments on certain issues.

Personal Experiences and Families

The majority of students (101 = 57.1 %) had not had significant lived experiences related to social or political issues. A relatively small number of students (30 = 16.9 %) had had such experiences; for example, the ongoing territorial disputes with neighboring countries, particularly China, and the timely topic of the raise of the consumption (value-added) tax from 5 % to 8 %. Forty-four (24.9 %) replied that they did not remember.

Youth stated that they were concerned with the issues if they had reasons to believe that such issues would affect their lives directly, such as the national pension plan, consumption-tax rates, and the increase of part-timers (or the decrease of full-time jobs). They will soon start paying premiums for the national pension plan, while the plan is expected to be in a big trouble by the time they receive their part because of the decrease in the number of working-age people who support the retired. Even before—far before retirement—they are worried about their job prospects.

Twenty-nine percent of the students stated that their families were politically active in some way (voting, discussing, etc.) and 20.3 % said their families were not. A significant portion of the students (50.3 %) replied they did not know.

Social and Political Participation

Overall, Japanese youth today are, like youth in other wealthy economies, not politically active—probably even less engaged or even more apathetic. For example, only 40.5 % (32 out of 79 students) of those who were voting age (20 years and up) answered that they voted,[4] and only 18.6 % of all participants said that they volunteered. Except for these two forms of participation and news following, their civic participation was almost negligible; those who had engaged in boycotting or protesting, joined political parties, or wrote to government officials were less than 2 % except for 9.0 % for protesting.

When we turn our eyes to their self-descriptions of how active youth are, only 2 people (1.1 %) stated they were "very active" in civic processes, 16 (9.0 %) "somewhat active", and 41 (23.2 %) "occasionally active", while 73 (41.2 %) stated they were "not very active" and 32 (18.1 %) "not active or interested". In other words, youth are twice as likely to be inactive than active.

We need to be a bit cautious about their self-descriptions of active involvement or interest. Even when they replied they were "active" to varying degrees (59 = 33.3 %), only 32.2 % of them voted and 33.9 % of them volunteered. News following seems to be the only activity in which many of them engaged (49.7 %), but 50.5 % of those who replied that they were "not very active" or "not active or interested" followed news as well; what this part of the survey shows seems to be merely the fact that TV watching is a popular activity after all (71.8 % of the students replied that they watched TV, and about 55 % of those who watched TV followed news).

Participants gave various reasons for not being active, such as they had other things to do (college classes, social life, job hunting, etc.), they were not interested or did not find politics and social issues relevant to their lives, or they felt powerless.

A few of these reasons deserve further consideration in the Japanese context. One is that some of them had not yet reached voting age. A second is that they did not feel that one person's voice or vote would count much (a sense of "external inefficacy"; [Takahashi, 2014, p. 79]). The third reason is that they felt their knowledge was inadequate for making social or political decisions ("internal inefficacy"; [Takahashi, 2014, p. 79]).

The first reason may be alleviated with the lowering of the voting age from 20 to 18. In my survey, 12 students wrote that they were not active in democratic processes because they had not yet reached the voting age (12.4 % of 97 students who were 18 or 19). Some critics, however, are rather skeptical about the prospect of an increased turnout among young voters because the overall pattern in Japan has been lower turnout among youth and somewhat higher turnout for people in their 30s and up (e.g. Hueston, 2015; Ishibashi, 2010; Soga, 2013). This has been consistently the case since universal suffrage was achieved after the Second World War (Soga, 2013).

In the survey, 13 students wrote that they were not active in democratic processes because they did not believe their voice or votes would have much influence; 17 stated that they were uninterested; 8 stated that they had other concerns. For example:

I am occupied with what's in front of me. I understand that such activities [involvement in democratic processes] are important, but I don't feel I have enough mental energy to
 spare. (student #64)
 My action alone won't change anything. (student #71)
 Those who are concerned should do it. I have other things to do. (student #156)

On the other hand, I find it interesting that about the same number of participants said that they did not know enough; among those who replied that they were not very active or even apathetic (105 = 59.3 % when both replies are combined), at least a dozen answered this way. Replies included:

I like to get involved, but don't have sufficient knowledge. (student #66)

I want to know and I feel I need to know because it is relevant to myself, but I feel it hard to start doing something because there are too many difficult things. (student #91)

I don't understand politics well, and I don't feel things will change significantly even if I

get interested. (student #130)

I think this comes, at least in part, from what Japanese schools do, or don't do, with regard to citizenship education.

In the classroom and through textbooks, Japanese junior and senior high school students learn who's who in the development of democracy, so to speak (e.g. Montesquieu wrote *The Spirit of the Laws* and proposed the separation of powers), but never read even a paragraph from their books. Being simply able to identify the correct author of a book and his or her famous idea when given choices or brackets in an exam is considered sufficient. They also learn the names of prime ministers and political parties, but they seldom study their political principles and agendas, let alone have chances to appraise them.

Thus, though Japanese schools, primarily in social studies classes, provide such *words* as democracy, human rights, division of power, parliamentary system, etc., they fail to teach *concepts*; I suspect that *Japanese youth are weak in forming relevant concepts to participate in civic processes in a usable way in real-life situations*—this is the hypothesis I propose which needs further examination.

Interestingly, 12 of those who replied positively about their experiences in social studies courses stated that the classes were interesting or useful because they helped them understand the news. On the other hand, some of those who found the classes uninteresting or useless stated that the classes had not been taught in a way that would help them deal with real issues (e.g. "We only read textbooks and I didn't understand how relevant the class would be to our lives." [student #142]).

Knowing certain *words* is not the same as having *concepts* expressed in such words. Even if one knows the distinction between capitalism and communism and is able to fill appropriate brackets in an exam, that does not guarantee she can understand what choosing democracy over communism would entail or how voting for a democratic party rather than for a communist party in her community would affect her everyday life. In order to acquire *concepts* as our intellectual tools to be used when necessary, we need to have chances to actually apply them in examining and discussing real issues. When Bernard Crick (2000) writes, "The teacher's task is, at whatever level, primarily a conceptual one, not a matter of conveying an agreed corpus of factual information" (p. 27), I think he is referring to this distinction. In this sense, Japanese social studies education is merely giving "an agreed corpus of factual information", and the fact that many students indicate that social studies classes were primarily about memorization testifies to my observation. From the social constructionist perspective (Chap. 1), it is hard to believe that students are acquiring or creating relevant knowledge in school because they are not encouraged to have interactive experiences.

In Japan, particularly in secondary schools, memorization of factual information is the *sine qua non* of education. Even though we now have "the period of integrated study" from the elementary school to senior high school, whose primary purpose is to "develop [students'] ability to learn and think independently and foster creativity" (Murata & Yamaguchi, 2010, p. 565), projects, discussions, and essays are still rare in the secondary school. In my study, only a few students reported having experienced such activities in school.

Views of Government/Democracy

Seventy-two percent of the students felt that social and political participation was either "important" or "somewhat important". Sixty-two percent said that they were either "very interested" or "somewhat interested" in the politics in Japan, and 44.1 % said that they were either "very interested" or "somewhat interested" in democracy in general.

Their reasons are interesting. Many students who said that it was important to participate in politics gave the reasons at the level of obligations or ethics; for example, it is only natural for a citizen to participate in the government of his/her country, or voting is a civic duty.

On the whole, many youth said that they valued democracy and that civic participation was important, but considering the fact that a lot less people were interested in actually getting involved, I wonder whether they genuinely thought so. It also seems likely that some of them will pick up interests and become more involved as they get older and established in work and community as a statistical survey on voter turnouts according to age groups over the past 50 years show.[5]

CORRELATIONS

I did not find strong correlations between either internal factors ("Self" in our model discussed in Chap. 1, e.g. personality types, the sense of self-efficacy) or external factors ("Context", e.g. ethnic/cultural background) on the one hand and political engagement on the other. The only exceptions were, first, whether youth had personally experienced political issues around them, and second, though to a much lesser degree, whether they had politically active family members, both of which are in the "context" category. On the surface of it, education and culture too seem to have correlations with political engagement; however, all participants in my survey were Japanese and all were supposed to have taken courses on citizenship education.

Personality types might be related with some types of political engagement; among the four types of personality I used in my survey (assertive/competitive, amiable/spontaneous, expressive/humanistic, and analytical/methodical), those who identified themselves as amiable/spontaneous were more likely to vote, but there were not such correlations with other types of civic participation. The correlation is not consistent enough to allow for generalization.

Ideally, the school makes the link between internal factors and contextual factors, enabling the youth to process the event they witnessed or experienced through their current civic mindset. They act on the basis of this cognition and receive feedback from the action, which in turn would help to shape their action in the future (Chap. 1). In the case of Japanese youth, the school, particularly the high school, does not seem to be functioning well in this cyclical mechanism, by not encouraging youth to test or act on their knowledge by examining real social issues.

Political Experience-Active Involvement

Fifty-seven percent of those who had encountered what they felt as pressing issues in their community or nation replied they were either "very active", "somewhat active", or "occasionally active", while 25.7 % of those who had not had such experiences and 36.4 % of those who did not remember were active.

Family-Active Involvement

About half of the students did not know whether their parents or siblings were politically active. Seventeen (34.0 %) of those who stated that their family members were active in politics were either "very active", "somewhat active", or "occasionally active", while eight students (22.2 %) whose family members were not active defined themselves as active to various degrees. On the other hand, 58.0 % of the students with politically active family members were not active themselves, and 72.2 % of the students whose family were not politically active were not themselves active. There seems to be a slight tendency for those from active families to be active themselves.

RECOMMENDATIONS

My observation is that the most serious problem of Japanese youth is their conceptual weakness, and I suggest that it is the *cause* of their disengagement with social and political issues; it is not that they do not know because they are uninterested, as typically assumed. Their replies on their social status and cultural identities seem to indicate their lack of knowledge or unfamiliarity with such issues; many replied that they did not know or wrote something irrelevant. We may interpret this as relative nonexistence of such issues of class and ethnicity in Japan, but these issues are certainly present (though, perhaps, not as significant as in North America or in Europe) and are reported daily in news programs—Remember news following is a popular activity.

Not large in number, perhaps, but some Japanese youth are indeed deeply concerned about their futures, both immediate and far, and are feeling insecure. At the same time, unfortunately, they do not know what they may be able to do to cope with these problems. Schools do not seem to be responding to their concerns, and in many cases, youth turn instead to news programs on TV or the information on the net for explanations and answers. One of the interviewees said that the reason he found the classes at school useless or uninteresting was that they dealt rather with historical issues and not contemporary issues. I think his statement is justified considering the curriculum and dominant teaching methods; not necessarily historical, perhaps, but at least theoretical or formal aspects are emphasized while discussion of and inquiry into contemporary divisive issues are avoided.

Japanese schools are under the tight control of the Ministry of Education, Culture, Sports, Science and Technology, and they seem to be unwilling to allow students to have open-ended discussions and inquiry into current political issues for fear of (mis-)leading youth to certain political standpoints. Thus, schools stick with imparting "basic" knowledge and, as a consequence, fail to equip youth with useful tools to handle socio-political issues that potentially have some bearings on their personal lives. In short, they are not taught in an empowering way (see Chap. 1). Concepts are powerful tools to understand and to deal with issues but they do not become intellectual tools unless students use them to see their powers and limitations in forming and defending their own ideas and arguments. Only by engaging in discussions on real issues, and considering the logical consequences of taking certain stands, will students get to understand (or "appreciate" in Dewey's [1916] term) usable concepts.

Anything can be made interesting (Egan, 2010) but when one lacks knowledge and conceptual tools to deal with issues, interest will be lacking. I think this is largely the case with Japanese youth.

In light of these observations, my major recommendation for Japanese schools is to use more project-style approaches that allow students to explore issues of their interest. The way we currently teach does not have to be the only way. There are alternative methods—*tsuzuri-kata*, for example, which I mentioned earlier being one of them—and some of them have even been practiced successfully in Japanese classrooms before.

Of course, it would be too optimistic to assume that the mere use of project-style learning by itself would enhance youth's social engagement and participation in Japan—after all, youth's disengagement is also a problem in such countries as the USA and Canada which have a stronger tradition of using such methods. However, there are a certain number of Japanese youth who are potentially willing to get involved, and what they need to actually do so seems to be to have opportunities in school to test out their knowledge and ideas with real issues.

NOTES

1. I thank my colleague for allowing me to conduct the survey in his class.
2. The Ministry of Education, Culture, Sports, Science and Technology's webpage: http://www.mext.go.jp/component/b_menu/other/__ics-Files/afieldfile/2015/08/18/1360722_01_1_1.pdf
3. Calculated from the data on the university's webpage (http://www.kokugakuin.ac.jp/).
4. My results are similar to, for example, the voter turnout for people in their 20s in the last two elections for the Lower House of the Diet (37.89 % in the election in December 2012 and 32.58 % in December 2014; the Association for Promoting Fair Elections, www.akaruisenkyo.or.jp/070various/071syugi/693/).
5. Voter turnouts of the people in their 30s and 40s are consistently 10 to 20 % higher than those of people in their 20s in the past 50 years. Turnouts become higher as people get older until they get to 60s, and become some-

what lower when they reach 70s, but this is probably for physical and health reasons. The Association for Promoting Fair Elections, http://www.akaruisenkyo.or.jp/070various/071syugi/693/

References

Benjamin, G. (1997). *Japanese lessons: A year in a Japanese school through the eyes of an American anthropologist and her children*. New York/London: New York University Press.

Crick, B. (2000). *Essays on citizenship*. London/ New York: Continuum Intl Pub Group.

Dewey, J. (1985/1916). *Democracy and education*. In J. A. Boydston (Ed.), *The middle works, 1899–1924* (Vol. 9). Carbondale, IL: The Southern Illinois University Press.

Egan, K. (2010). *Learning in depth: A simple innovation that can transform schooling*. Chicago, IL: The University of Chicago Press.

Freire, P. (1970/1993). *Pedagogy of the oppressed*. (M. B. Ramos, Trans.). New York: Continuum.

Fujiwara, T. (2011). International, global and multicultural education as an issue in citizenship education. In N. Ikeno (Ed.), *Citizenship education in Japan* (pp. 107–115). New York: Continuum.

Horio, T. (1995). *Nihon no kyoiku (Education in Modern Japan)*. Tokyo: Tokyo University Press (In Japanese).

Hueston, D. (2015, July 2). Will lower voting age bring youth to polls? *The Japan Times*. Retrieved from http://www.japantimes.co.jp/news/2015/07/02/national/politics-diplomacy/will-lower-voting-age-bring-youths-polls/#.Vt6Kzcd0Xrk

Ikeno, N. (Ed.) (2011). *Citizenship education in Japan*. New York: Continuum.

Ishikawa, S. (2010). Citizenship to kankyo kyoiku (Citizenship and environmental education). In A. Nakayama et al. (Eds.), *Citizenship e no kyoiku* (Education for citizenship) (pp. 33–64). Tokyo: Shinyo-sha (In Japanese).

Ishibashi, S. (2010). Koukousei no seiji-teki yukouseikankaku ni kansuru kenkyu (A study on high school students' sense of political efficacy). *Social capital to Shimin sanka (Social capital and Civic participation)* (pp. 69–94). Kansai University: Institute of Economic and Political Studies.

Kodama, S. (2010). *Citizenship no kyoiku shiso (Educational thought of citizenship)*. Tokyo: Hakutaku-sha (In Japanese).

Kokubun, I. (1955). Afterword to Seikyo Muchaku, *Yamabiko Gakko* (Echoes from a Mountain School). Tokyo: Iwanami Shoten, (In Japanese).

Lewis, C. (1995). *Educating hearts and minds: Reflections on Japanese preschool and elementary education*. New York: Cambridge University Press.

Matsuno, O. (1997). *Kindai nohon no koumin kyoiku: kyokasho no naka no jiyuu, hou, kyousou* (Citizenship education in modern Japan: Freedom, law, and competition in textbooks), Nagoya: University of Nagoya Press (In Japanese).

Ministry of Education, Culture, Sports, Science and Technology. (2008). *Chugakko gakushu shido youryou (The national course of study: Junior high school).* (In Japanese). Retrieved from http://www.mext.go.jp/a_menu/shotou/new-cs/youryou/chu/

Muchaku, S. (1953). *Echoes from a Mountain School* (G. Gaulfield & M. Kimura, Trans.). Tokyo: Kenkyusha.

Muchaku, S. (1997). *Yamabiko gakko.* Tokyo: Iwanami Shoten Original Work Published in 1951.

Murata, Y., & Yamaguchi, M. (Eds.) (2010). *A bilingual text education in contemporary Japan: System and content.* Tokyo: Toshindo.

Nakayama, A., Ishikawa, S., Mori, M., Morita, E., Suzuki, M., & Sonoda, M. (2010). *Citizenship e no kyoiku (Education for citizenship).* Tokyo: Shinyo-sha (In Japanese).

NHK Broadcasting, Culture Research Institute (2015). *Gendai Nihonjin no ishiki kozo (The mental structure of contemporary Japanese).* Tokyo: NHK Books (In Japanese).

Report of the United States Education Mission to Japan (1946). Washington, DC: U. S. Government Printing Office.

Rohlen, T. (1983). *Japan's high schools.* Berkeley and Los Angeles: University of California Press.

Soga, T. (2013, August 11). The decline of youth' voting rates: Instead of whining 'young people these days are…'. *The Asashi Shinbun,* p. 7. (In Japanese).

Takahashi, S. (2014). Daigaku ni okeru citizenship kyoiku no tameno yobiteki kousatsu (A preliminary examination of citizenship education in university). *Shakai-Kagaku Kyoiku Nenpo, 44,* 185–189 (In Japanese).

The Advisory Group on Citizenship (1998). *Education for citizenship and the teaching of democracy in schools final report of the advisory group on citizenship.* London: Qualification and Curriculum Authority.

Tsurumi, K. (1995). Afterword to Seikyo Muchaku, *Yamabiko Gakko (Echoes from a Mountain School).* Tokyo: Iwanami Shoten. (In Japanese)

UNESCO (1998). *World declaration on higher education for the twenty-first century: Vision and action.* Paris: UNESCO. Retrieved from http://www.unesco.org/education/educprog/wche/declaration_eng.htm.

Yamazumi, M. (1995). Afterword to Masako Toyoda, *Tsuzurikata Kyoshitsu (Tsuzurikata classroom).* Tokyo: Iwanami Shoten (In Japanese).

Yamazumi, M. (1997). *Sensou to kyouiku (Japan's wars and education).* Tokyo: Iwanami Shoten (In Japanese).

Yamazumi, M. (2007). *Nihon kyouiku sho-shi: kinn-genndai* (A brief history of Japanese education in the modern and contemporary eras). Tokyo: Iwanami Shoten (In Japanese).

CHAPTER 8

Exploring Youth Civic Engagement and Disengagement in Mexico

Medardo Tapia Uribe

As in other countries of Latin America, Mexico's concern with citizenship education is related to the social and democratic crises that Mexico has experienced. Citizenship Education as Peace Education has evolved following the development of war, peace and social conflicts worldwide and the long aspiration for democracy and democratic governments. As Chile launched a strong citizenship education program related to human rights due to the human rights crisis they live through during Pinochet's *coup d'état* and dictatorship, Mexico's long undemocratic, one-party rule, for more than 70 years, gave birth to political reform followed by educational reform and later citizenship education reform. One of our first contemporary social and democratic crises has been acknowledged to have been in 1968, a student social movement that ended up with the Tlatelolco massacre on October 2. Many politicians and specialists agree that this might have been the beginning of several political reforms in Mexico. It was behind a new 1976 education law and political reform in 1977, which

M.T. Uribe (✉)
Gobierno y Políticas Públicas, Centro Regional de Investigaciones
Multidisciplinarias, Universidad Nacional Autónoma de México, Cuernavaca,
Morelos, México
e-mail: medardo@unam.mx

© The Author(s) 2017
C. Broom (ed.), *Youth Civic Engagement in a Globalized World*,
Palgrave Studies in Global Citizenship Education and Democracy,
DOI 10.1057/978-1-137-56533-4_8

opened the door to a multiparty system. The results of the 1988 presidential elections, despite a questionable Partido Revolucionario Institucional victory, gave birth to the 1993 General Law of Education (Morfín, 1993) and 1996 Mexican Political Reform. This last political reform gave and left election processes in an autonomous citizen council. These political and educational reforms produced a new citizenship education program for junior high school—1999 at the *secundaria* level. They are important for understanding youth civic engagement in Mexico. Despite these reforms and new citizenship education programs for primary and high schools, released a few years later, one of the latest national studies on citizenship found that youngsters between 18 and 29 years of age least participate in non-electoral political activities (Vaquero, Galván, & Morales, 2014). This is also the age group that does not vote and 52 % of them do not identify with any political party. Similarly, Latinobarómetro (2015) reported that Mexico ranked at the bottom of 18 Latin American countries in terms of its satisfaction with democracy; only 19 % of Mexicans are satisfied with it.

Before the 1999 citizenship education program, *Civic and Ethics Education* (*Formación Cívica y Ética*), the old *Civics Education* program (*Educación Cívica*) emphasized nationalism and a sort of uncritical loyalty to the Mexican State. Knowledge, skills and attitudes were the parameters chosen by the Mexican program for citizenship and ethics education for grades 7 through 9 (Mexico's Ministry of Education, 2004). The Mexican program decided to articulate these citizenship education parameters around what they called three formative axes: life formation, citizenship formation and ethics formation. Additionally, the following eight themes are utilized, spanning from the more personal aspects of students' lives to broader spheres of participation and social interaction: knowledge and care of oneself, "auto regulation" and responsible exercise of freedom, respect and value of diversity, a sense of belonging to a community, nation and humanity, management and conflict resolution, political and social participation, respect for the law and a sense of justice, and an understanding and evaluation of democracy.

At the end of their two courses of citizenship and ethics education, secondary school graduates should be able to assess the human rights and values that society has created as well as attitudes to the denunciation of human rights violations that society has developed. Graduates should also be trained to respect and honor promises made to themselves and others, value their participation on personal and collective matters of democratic life, and manage and solve conflicts without violence by means of dialogue and consensus-building. Students should also be able, in this formative process, to build a positive self-image by acknowledging their own history, interests, potentials and capacities as autonomous people and dignified human beings, who are capable of making responsible decisions that empower them and allow them to identify conditions and alternatives for the short-, medium- and long-term future. In this same formative process, students should also learn to value Mexico's cultural diversity and acknowledge what they share with others by respecting differences and plurality as principles of a democratic way of life. Students must also be able to identify and understand democracy, federalism, the electoral system and procedures of democratic participation, as well as to assume democratic principles for themselves.[1]

Most of the young Mexicans in our sample, between the ages of 18 and 29, were subject to this kind of citizenship education program. They were at least at junior high school, grades 7th, 8th and 9th when the new program was enacted.

Nevertheless, several empirical studies have found that Mexican Citizenship Education has been unsuccessful against a prevailing non-democratic political culture, which is more powerful and successful than the basic education programs. Araújo-Olivera et al. (2005), in a sample of 22 junior high schools (*secundarias*), found that students were socialized under a concept of politics in which "someone else decides for us", that citizenship means "some has more rights than others" and that democracy is "to vote to choose our government representatives" (p. 37). Students express a deep rejection of politics because they consider it corrupt and linked to violence and conflict (Araújo-Olivera et al., 2005).

Another citizenship and environment education study of 2158 *Secundaria* and High School Students (*Bachillerato*) and citizens of Cuernavaca, Morelos in Mexico found programs end up setting "awareness" as the learning achievement goal, putting aside citizenship knowledge, skills and values (Tapia, 2016). Nevertheless, there is interest on the part of students to engage in local environment problems. However, they are not very hopeful of achieving their goals as citizens. Students also acknowledge they do not know how to organize themselves and participate as citizens (Tapia, 2016). Teachers insist on instructing their students without discussing real civic problems in class, those they see and live every day (Yurén, 2013).

METHODOLOGY

The study proposed to answer three questions:

- *What are the characteristics and features of youth civic engagement and disengagement in a pluralistic democracy?*
- *How does engagement relate to individual characteristics and experiences?*
- *If disengagement is found, what are its forms (types) and causes and what can be done about it?*

For this we interviewed a sample of 184 youngsters between 18 and 29 years of age, in three Mexican cities, one in the central part of Mexico and two in northern cities. Cuernavaca and Ciudad Juarez are known for their high rates of violence in recent years, and the other northern city in Sonora does not have these violence rates. Although we did not do a random sample, we looked for contrasting regions of Mexico as well as different socioeconomic levels, including different levels of schooling. Almost half of our sample, 47.9 %, were between 18 and 20 years of age, 31.5 % were between 21 and 24 and 20.6 % were between 25 and 29 years of age. A total of 74.5 % were from Cuernavaca, Morelos, one hour drive south of Mexico City; 14.7 % were from Ciudad Juárez, Chihuahua on the northern border of Mexico with the USA and 10.9 % were from Hermosillo, the capital of the state of Sonora, in the northern part of Mexico.

Half of our sample were women and men; 75 % were university students; 4.4 % had high school schooling and 19.5 % had *secundaria* or less schooling. Most of our interviewees identified themselves as working class, 47.8 % as middle class and only 1.1 % as high social class. Some of our questions on our survey were open ended.

RESULTS

One indicator of youth civic engagement is the political or social activities that they engage in, in addition to participation in elections and voting. Our results show that most of the youngsters in our sample, outside of school or work, never join political parties, get involved in "issues", talk about politics or participate in any "patriotic" activities. The most promising youth civic engagement activities are participation in community work, even though 54.3 % of the youth responded that they never engage in this kind of activity. A recent national survey of Mexican Citizenship Quality confirmed our findings (Vaquero et al., 2014). This survey found that youth between 18 and 29 years of age participate less in non-electoral political activities than other age groups.

The civic processes that Mexican youth engage in can be divided into two kinds. Those civic processes in which more than half of the youth participate: voting, volunteering, donating money to causes, helping those in need and participating in their local community. It looks as if actions of solidarity and local community needs call Mexican youth to engage in civic activities because of their observable immediate results and perhaps because of youth's lack of trust in Mexican political institutions. Helping those in need was the civic process that most Mexican youth would engage in (84.8 %), even more than voting (71.8 %), followed by participation in their local community (66.8 %). This might mean that trying to contribute to solve local social issues is more attractive than engaging in civic processes. Perhaps this is why volunteering is also a preferred civic process to engaging in and donating money to causes. Mexican youth seems to consider that solidarity, benefiting the community and contributing to social changes in the community are better reasons for engaging in civic processes than those of joining political parties or civic organizations.

Those civic processes that require youth to join an organization and groups or a political party are not attractive to Mexican youngsters, nor are writing to government officials or newspapers or participating in political discussions using social media. Almost 87 % of youth (86.6 %) and 86.7 % would never engage in discussions using social media or boycotting. These are the least attractive civic processes youth would engage in, followed by joining a political party: 78 % of youth would never join a political party.

In trying to answer our second research question, we analyzed the relationship between "Civic Processes Youth Engage in" and the civic education they learned in *secundaria* and high school. We analyzed first this relationship among those civic processes that more than 50 % of youth engaged in (voting, volunteering, and donating money to causes, helping those in need and participating in their local community). We found that all of these associations were statistically significant, that is, there was a covariation, except for the relationship between "...civic education..." and "helping those in need". The significant association between "Learning Civic Education..." and "...Voting" means that those youth who learned civic education voted more than those who did not have it or did not remember it. This is also true for the association between "...civic education…" and "…volunteering": those youth who learned civic education volunteered more than those youth who did not learn civic education or do not remember learning it.

We also found this kind of statistically significant association between youth that learned "Civic Education" and those who engaged in "Donating money to causes": those youth that learned civic education donated money to causes more than those who did not learn civic education or did not remember it. Finally, we also found a statistically significant association between learning civic education and participating in their local community: those youth that learned civic education participated in their local community more than their counterparts who did not learn civic education or did not remember it.

To add answers to our second research question, we analyzed the relationship between how active youth were and the civic processes they engaged in. We found that the first variable, how active youth were, was significantly associated with helping those in need, volunteering, voting, donating money to causes and participating in their local community. In general, this means that those youth that are more active tend to participate more in these specific civic processes.

We found another statistically significant association between the importance youth assigned to people's involvement in improving their communities and helping those in need and participating in their local community.

These associations developed a pattern that led us to hypothesize that those youth who are more active and engaged in these civic processes are also those that rate themselves more knowledgeable, were raised within active political families, think their actions can bring change to society, join political parties and have had significant "political" experiences that have affected their view of politics. We tested these and some other variables like the news youth listen to. We found a positive and significant association between "How Knowledgeable would You Rate Yourself in Politics…" and "Civic Process: Voting". This means that those Mexican youth that rate themselves more knowledgeable engage more in voting than their counterparts who are less knowledgeable. There was also a significant association between "How knowledgeable…" and "Civic Process… Donating Money to Causes", "Civic Process… Joining a Political Party", "How active are you in the civic processes…", "Significant experience…", "When you were growing up… family active in political…" This means that those Mexican youth that rate themselves knowledgeable or with some knowledge engage more in the civic processes we have listed, are more active in civic processes, have had more politically significant experiences that change their view of politics and were raised in more politically active families than those youth who rated themselves to have little knowledge of politics and government (see Table 8.1). Unfortunately, we need more research to evaluate which of these two variables is stronger: having had an active political family or civic education.

We also hypothesized that several variables, like having grown up within an active political family, would be powerful influences on youth attitudes, views and engagement in several civic processes. We found a significant association between "When you were growing up... family active in political activities..." and "How effective... your actions... can change... your society", "Civic processes you engage in... voting", "Civic processes... volunteering", "Civic processes... interacting political... using social media", "Civic processes... joining a political party", "How active are you in... civic processes" and "...Any significant experiences... community... government... politics that changed your views".

Another important variable whose influence we hypothesize as possibly significant was the importance youth assigned to be actively involved in improving their communities. We found a significant association between youth giving importance to this view of improving their communities and voting, their view of actions contributing to change their society, joining political parties, how active they should be in civic processes and having had a significant political experience that changed their views (see Table 8.1).

On these grounds of searching for variables that influence Mexican youth engagement in civic processes, we also analyzed the hypothetical influence upon their political activities and their engagement of certain civic processes on other civic processes. Our results show that youth engagement in political activities (joining political parties, talking about politics and getting involved in issues) is the most power influence upon the other civic processes that Mexican youth engage in. Engagement in political activities is significantly associated with other civic processes youth engage in: voting, volunteering, interacting in political activities, helping those in need, joining a political party, degree of activeness in civic processes, significant political experience and having grown up in a family politically active.

The other variables that are influential upon other variables are the civic processes themselves that Mexican youth engage in: voting was significantly associated with interacting in political activities and discussions in social media, helping those in need, joining a political party,

Table 8.1　Significant associations between youth and civic behaviors in Mexico

	How active are you in the civic processes listed before?	How knowledgeable would you rate yourself on politics...	Family active political	How important... it is for people to be actively involved in improving their communities?
Civic process: Helping those in need	$\chi^2 = 21.124$ $\alpha = .000$ n =170			
Civic process: Volunteering	$\chi^2 = 20.439$ $\alpha = .000$ n =165		$\chi^2 = 5.8$ $\alpha = .05$ n = 141	
Civic process: Voting	$\chi 29$ $\alpha= .000$ n =169	$\chi^2 =4.01$ $\alpha = .04$ n = 170		$\chi^2 = 5.299$ $\alpha = .021$ n = 168
Civic process: Donating money to causes	$\chi 20$ $\alpha = .000$ n =165	χ $\alpha = .06$ n = 166		
Civic process: Participating in my local community	$\chi 77$ $\alpha = .000$ n =168			
Civic process: Joining a political party		χ $\alpha = .06$ n = 159	$\chi^2 = 8.5$ $\alpha = .014$ n = 134	
CP: Interacting in political... activities or discussions using social media			$\chi^2 = 3.1$ $\alpha = .07$ n = 140	
Activities: Political join political parties, talk about politics, get involved in issues				$\chi^2= 5.402$ $\alpha = .020$ n = 167
How active are you in the civic processes listed before?		$\chi^2 = .004$ n = 179	$\chi^2 = 19.01$ $\alpha = .000$ n = 151	$\chi^2 = 5.998$ $\alpha = .014$ n = 177
How effective... your actions can be to bring change to your society?			$\chi^2\alpha = .03$ N= 149	χ^2 $\alpha = .000$ n = 176
Significant Experience		χ $\alpha = .005$ n = 151	$\chi^2 = 2.8$ $\alpha = .09$ n = 129	$\chi 8$ $\alpha = .035$ n = 149
Family active political		$\chi^2 = 9.93$ $\alpha = .002$ n = 155		

Source: Our own survey 2015

degree of activity in civic processes and significant experience. However, it is not clear if engaging in voting might influence the other civic processes Mexican youth engage in or if it is the opposite.

Among these relationships between civic processes Mexican youth engage in, we also found volunteering significantly associated with interacting, helping those in need, joining a political party, level of activity in civic processes, significant experience and once again family's level of political activity. In other words, those Mexican youth that participate in volunteering are also more politically active. This might be related to having been raised in a family that is more politically active.

Youth interaction in political/social activities or discussions using social media was significantly associated with joining a political party, level of activity in civic processes, having had a significant political experience that changed their views and having been raised in a politically active family. In this same kind of analysis, youth donating money to causes was significantly associated with helping those in need, joining a political party, level of activity in civic processes and having grown in a family that was politically active. Joining a political party was associated with youth level of activity in civic processes and having had a politically active family.

We analyzed the relationship between how supportive youth were of their country's government and several means of youth civic participation. We did not find any significant association. One of the reasons was that there were very few cases in this category. Most of those who do not support Mexico's government are strongly unsatisfied with its corruption, impunity, violence, lack of public security, and illegitimacy.

In contrast, we found that Mexican youth were supportive of democratic governments in general, 43 out of 176, whereas only 3 out of 159 were supportive of their own government. Mexican youth supported democracy in general because, according to our survey, it is the best political form to undertake social change.

Mexican youth, 48.3 % ($n = 184$), consider it important to participate in government processes, such as voting, boycotting, volunteering, protesting, and so on, whereas 14.6 % of youth do not think it is important to participate in these processes. In contrast, a larger percentage of Mexican youth (72.2 %) consider it more important to be actively involved in improving their communities than participating in such government processes; only 3.3 % consider it not important to be actively involved in their communities. They also tell us why it is important to be actively involved in improving their community: to engage collectively in improving the community, to build a better society, to build the society we wish, to work on something that affects all, to work on something we all know, to change the community in which we live, to work for changes that we know are feasible, to call to other members of the community, to lead others and to raise awareness of community needs and problems. We would need to do more research to understand where this strong focus on community comes from. It could be from Mexican religion or family and social values. It seems that the lack of trust in political institutions and government processes calls youth to work directly in their communities.

Most of those who decide not to engage in civic processes argue that they have no time; they are too busy at their jobs, school. Others argue that "everything is a lie... politicians rob to the country... politics is disgusting... I have lost faith on change".[2] Some of them stated that they are not taken into account because they are young and another group of youth simply admitted that they lacked knowledge of the political system.

Given youth's rejection of participation in such government processes, we analyzed whether they had had any significant community, government or political experiences that affected their views of politics or government and its association with how active they were in such civic processes. We found that only 26.8 % of Mexican youth had had such experiences and that there was a significant association between having had such experiences and how active they were. Those significant experiences, according to Mexican youth, are corrupt electoral processes (buying of citizen's votes), witnessing government physical violence and repression, unfulfilled promises, politicians' self-interest and neighbors' apathy for engaging in civic processes. These results perhaps confirm why youth focus on working directly in their communities.

We thought that these significant experiences might be related to youth's knowledge of politics. We analyzed this relationship and found that there was a significant association between these two variables, that is, those youth that rate themselves as more knowledgeable of politics and government have had more significant experiences than their counterparts with little knowledge.

We hypothesized that those youth with significant experiences, who are more knowledgeable of politics and more active in civic processes, are also those who are voting, helping those in need, participating in their local community, volunteering and those who have had civic education. We confirmed this: we found that there was a significant association between these variables. We need more research, putting all these variables into a single model to evaluate their contributions.

In addition, we also analyzed the association between youth's positive attitudes toward being actively involved in their communities and their participation in certain civic processes. We found a statistically significant association between the former and voting, participating in political activities (join political parties, talk about politics…) and having had significant community, government, or political experiences that affected their views. This means that those Mexican youth who are willing to be actively involved in their communities tend to vote, engage in political activities, have had a political significant experience that has affected their views and participate in their local communities.

This is the horizon of youth engaging in civic processes and participating in improving their communities. However, we also analyzed how effective Mexican youth consider their citizenship actions can be to bring change to their society. We found that 40.1 % of youth felt their actions could be effective to bring change to their society. When we examine if this is related to the different levels of importance they assign to being actively involved in civic processes and improving their communities, we found that some of these associations were significant. This means that those Mexican youth that consider their actions to be effective in bringing change to their society are more active than those that are not.

We also found that there is a significant association between those youth that believe that it is important to be actively involved in improving their communities and how effective they believe their actions can be to bring change in their society. Those that believe that is not important to be actively involved also tend to believe that their actions are not effective.

Finally, we found that only 36.4 % of Mexican youth regularly follow the news.

This low percentage was similar to the low percentages of youth engaging in other civic processes. Despite this, we decided to analyze if this association distinguished between those who engage in civic process and those who do not.

We found that "participating in my local community" is significantly associated with all of these youth civic processes. This means that youth who are participating in their local community are also following political news, joining civic groups, interacting in political activities and discussions using social media, good neighbors, getting involved in a cause, doing community work and participating in patriotic activities, more than those youth participating less in their local community. Another set of resulting significant associations was between youth engaging in "Writing government officials or newspapers" and following political news, protesting, joining civic groups [...], interacting [...] discussions using social media, getting involved in a cause and participating in patriotic activities.

There were also some other significant associations between youth following political news and other variables, like protesting, using social media for discussions and doing community work. This could mean that being active in one's community leads one to be more active politically too, or to feel a sense of efficacy to bring change. We also found that youth who engage in protesting also engage more in civic processes, like joining civic groups, getting involved in a cause and being a good neighbor than their counterparts that participate less in such civic processes.

CONCLUSIONS AND RECOMMENDATIONS

Mexico has been in a social and political crisis for several decades, and our transition to democracy is weak and unfinished. Some of the political reforms made in 1977 and 1996 attempted to contribute to such a transition as well as improve citizenship education. The latter, including the new civic and ethics education of *secundaria* (1999), as well as the primary and high school reforms, were a consequence of political reforms. Nevertheless, opposition parties and Mexican citizens have still profoundly questioned the last two presidential elections results. Several specialists and national leaders have also argued that we have not had a democratic transition. Research on the new civics and ethics programs has indicated some of its shortcomings. Other national surveys have also found that Mexican youth are in the age cohort with the lowest level of participation in elections and other civic processes.

Nevertheless, our first finding and the first feature of Mexican youth's civic engagement shows that civic education is associated, significantly, with those civic processes which youth engage in most, that is, voting, volunteering, donating money to causes, helping those in need and participating in their local community. This means that civic education does have an impact on youth in these specific civic processes, although not on others like joining a political party. We would need to do more research on this issue. We only know it is significant, but not how powerful it is. Mexican youth are engaging in civic processes where they can contribute to their local communities and help those in need directly. The illegitimacy of electoral processes and government corruption, they told us, are their reasons for not supporting the Mexican government. In contrast, we found that 96.4 % considered it important to be actively involved in improving their communities. This is relevant because this attitude is associated with other attitudes and civic processes—how effective… your actions can be to bring change to… society, engage in political activities, voting, level of activity in civic processes in general and to be more open to have significant experiences that changed their view. These associations are, in turn, important to other youth civic engagement features and processes. We do not know, as we said above, where this strong Mexican youth's focus on contributing to their community and helping those in need comes from. Mexican schools do not do community work. It might be more related to their lack of trust in political parties and organizations.

When we analyzed this particular form of Mexican youth civic engagement, especially in these specific civic processes, we found a pattern: those youth that rate themselves as more knowledgeable, that grew up in families that were politically active, that think that their actions can change their society and who have had "political" experiences that have changed their views, were also more active in engaging in civic processes than their counterparts without these features. These civic processes are voting, donating money to causes, joining a political party, volunteering, interacting in political/social activities or discussions using social media and participating their local community.

We also found significant associations among civic processes themselves. Those who vote and volunteer also engage in political/social activities and discussions using social media, help those in need and join a political party more than those who do not vote. In the same trend, those who engage more in "political/social activities…" tend to join a political party more than those who do not engage in "political/social activities"; and donating money to causes is associated with helping those in need and joining a political party. It seems that youth engagement in some civic processes strengthens their engagement in other civic processes. Or that active, empowered youth are active in many ways.

Finally, we tested a hypothesis that we would not find a significant association between those civic processes that youth engage in less than other civic processes: participating in my local community, following political news, joining civic groups, interacting in political activities and social discussion using social media, being a good neighbor, getting involved in a cause, community work, participating in patriotic activities, writing government officials or newspapers and protesting. In contrast to our hypothesis, we did find significant associations between most of these variables, with participating in my local community, following political news, writing government officials or newspapers, protesting and joining civic groups, being, apparently, the most powerful contributors to the rest of the youth civic processes and activities Mexican youth engage in, despite low levels of youth engagement in these civic processes.

In sum, having had a civic education and being raised in a family that was politically active are powerful contributors and influences upon youth's conceptions, knowledge, attitudes and experiences that can strengthen their level of activity in civic processes in general and specifically in voting and those socially focused activities, like volunteering, donating money and helping those in need, that improve their communities. Youth civic engagement is possible despite youth's rejection and lack of support for a government that they consider to be illegitimate, corrupt and repressive. We do not have enough elements in this research to measure whether family or education contributes more to Mexican youth engagement in civic processes and activities.

We propose to improve civic education programs and youth civic education by inviting Mexican youth to engage in local community programs, like those that they engage in, even those with the lowest levels of engagement. We propose to make these programs part of their *secundaria* and high school civic education. We also propose to offer them, as is being done, in Colombia and Brazil, citizen schools, *Escuelas Ciudadanas*. However, it must be emphasized that the content of these civic education programs would be real problems in their communities, rather than abstract problems. Youth prefer to be educated as citizens working on real politically and social problems. We cannot go further into expanding these recommendations without more research and a larger report.

NOTES

1. Part of these arguments was published in: Tapia Uribe, Medardo, in "Citizenship and Peace Education," in *International Security, Peace, Development and Environment. Book 39 of Encyclopedia of Life Support Systems*, ed. Ursula Oswald (Oxford, United Kingdom: UNESCO and Oxford University Press, 2006), 14.
2. Answer to open-ended question number 15.

REFERENCES

Araújo-Olivera, S., Yurén Camarena, M. T., Estrada Ruiz, M. J., & Cruz Reyes, M. (2005). Respeto, democracia y política. Negación del Consenso: El caso de la formación cívica y ética en escuelas secundarias de Morelos. *Revista Mexicana de Investigación Educativa, 10*(24), 15–42.

Latinobarómetro. (2015). *Opinión pública Latinoamericana. Informe 1995–2015.* Banco de datos en línea. www.latinobarómetro.org. Accessed September 29, 2015.

Mexico's Ministry of Education (2004). *Propuesta preliminar de los programas de formación cívica y ética.* Mexico City: Secretaría de Educación Pública.

Morfín, L. (1993). Introducción. In *Comentarios a la Ley General de Educación.* Ciudad de México: Centro de Estudios Educativos, A. C.

Tapia Uribe, M. (2016). *Cuernavaca. Formación ciudadana y ambiental en la escuela y la acción ciudadana.* Cuernavaca, Morelos: Centro Regional de Investigaciones Multidisciplinarias, Universidad Nacional Autónoma de México.

Vaquero Otero, L. J., Galván, S. & Morales Camarena F. J., Coordinadores. (2014). *Informe país sobre la calidad de la ciudadanía en México.* Ciudad de México: Instituto Nacional Electoral y El Colegio de México.

Yurén, T. (2013). *Ciudadanía y educación. Ideales, dilemas y posibilidades de la formación ético-política.* Ciudad de México: Juan Pablos Editores y Universidad Autónoma del Estado de Morelos.

CHAPTER 9

Youth Engagement or Disengagement, Civic Mindsets, and Democracy

Tania Naanous and Catherine Broom

This book began by elaborating a model of youth attitudes and behaviors toward civic life that was dynamic and fluid. It theorized that youth's attitudes and actions were the product of the interaction of their internal and external factors, which create a particular civic mindset in youth. Internal factors are considered to be such elements as personality traits, attitudes, knowledge, and feelings of efficacy. External elements include school, family, and culture. As these factors continually play on each other and influence individuals and their sense making, and consequently, actions,

---

The Mexico Peace Research Center is an Academic team that emerges from Iberoamericana University in Mexico City. Their main work is dedicated to qualitative analysis and research of topics related to violence and peace construction in Mexico. In addition, it works actively on projects that involve connecting with people around the world who can provide knowledge about peace to Mexican society.

T. Naanous
Mexico Peace Research Center, Mexico City, Mexico

C. Broom (✉)
Faculty of Education, University of British Columbia Okanagan,
Kelowna, BC, Canada
e-mail: catherine.broom@ubc.ca

© The Author(s) 2017
C. Broom (ed.), *Youth Civic Engagement in a Globalized World*,
Palgrave Studies in Global Citizenship Education and Democracy,
DOI 10.1057/978-1-137-56533-4_9

youth's civic mindsets and behaviors were theorized to be continually constructed and emerging.

In subsequent chapters, we explored this model in seven nations/societies with varied experiences with democracy. In this chapter, we summarize the major findings and relate them back to this model. We also draw on a case study discussion of one nation by Tania Naanous to discuss the challenges and possibilities of citizenship education in the twenty-first century.

REVIEWING THE MODEL

Across the seven nations/societies in which the research was carried out, connections were found between some internal and external factors and youth's civic attitudes and behaviors. In most of the nations/societies studied, and as has been much discussed by many scholars, youth civic engagement was limited, in the traditional civic, social, and political sense (Marshall, 1950). Youth described their engagement as primarily "occasionally active" and the ways in which they were active focused around "traditional activities" such as voting and volunteering (Bennett, Freelon, & Wells, 2010). Youth understood citizens to be individuals who contribute to their societies primarily under Marshall's (1950) social (volunteering, contributing to the public good) and political (voting) types of citizenship. Few youth were active in more transformative civic processes, such as boycotting or joining a political party or demonstration. Many youth also described themselves as having a limited sense of self-efficacy. Japanese youth, for example, stated that they were limited in their knowledge and engagement in civic life, mentioning that they lacked political knowledge and were focused on other priorities.

In Canada, however, the findings differed to those of the pilot (Broom, 2016), as youth stated they were more actively engaged and felt a sense of self-efficacy. This was due to a contextual factor: the study was held before, during and after an election which saw some of the highest voting numbers in history as Canadians were ready for a change in government from the long governance of Prime Minister Stephen Harper, who many felt had become too right wing. Canadian youth described themselves as having a high sense of self-efficacy to bring about change, as they voted in record numbers. They saw their votes lead to the election of Justin Trudeau, and thus they felt effective. Opportunity and action went hand-in-hand with an increased sense of self-efficacy.

In Hong Kong, youth demonstrated civic engagement through movements such as the Umbrella Movement, due to contextual factors there, related to political and civil changes associated with Hong Kong's handover to China. However, youth did not feel that their actions had much political effect, unlike Canadian youth, due to differing political contexts, and youth's perceptions of the impact of their actions.

Youth have the potential to be actively involved when they see it as relevant to themselves and are given opportunities to do so, that is, when the context is right. It is possible that youth's involvement is limited at other times when they do not see it is a high priority based on their interests and needs and when they are focused on other goals such as establishing their careers. Thus, civic engagement is dynamic and fluid as the model theorized. Youth appear to make decisions about whether they think civic or political participation is worth it or not, based on their contexts.

A number of nations around the world call themselves democracies but fail to live up to the elements necessary for democracy. In the chapter on Mexico, for example, the research study demonstrated that youth focus on participating in their communities and not on political engagement, as youth believe their government is corrupt and untrustworthy, describing vote buying and violence. Recently, BBC news reported government intimidation and house arrest of individuals running for office in Uganda (BBC, 2016).[1] When governments use practices such as intimidation, voting buying, or the curtailing of individuals' legal and human rights, democracy does not exist in practice. Civil rights, such as freedom of speech and legal rights, are necessary and essential for democracy (Marshall, 1950). When youth grow up in contexts where these are missing or curtailed, it makes sense that youth political involvement may be limited. Why would youth choose to be involved when they know that their votes are not real ones, or speak out if they might get hurt, intimidated, or otherwise punished for doing so? Youth perceptions of political corruption or politician untrustworthiness emerged in most of the nations surveyed; however, comments on the use of fear, intimidation, vote tampering, or lack of confidence in the process emerged in some countries more than others, particularly in nations that had more poverty. Corruption and fear may control behavior, but they do not create contexts in which civil society or democracy can flourish. In other nations, where civil rights are protected, these rights may be taken somewhat for granted. Youth should learn about these rights, both their historical development and contemporary manifestation, as well as learn to appreciate how essential they are to the civic culture necessary for democracy.

Returning to the model, the chapters in this book found that personality was not a key factor in youth's voting behaviors, although there were some connections between youth's self-perceptions of themselves as kind and volunteering. Knowledge and attitudes were related to civic behaviors. Generally, youth who had some political knowledge were more active. Political knowledge seems to lead to increased engagement and to recognition of the responsibilities that come with, as well as an appreciation for, democratic forms of government. Youth supported the belief that democracy requires people's participation.

Youth may participate more if they know more about it. Thus, we suggest that citizenship education continues to teach knowledge about democracy, government structures and processes, and civic attitudes and actions. However, as Keiichi Takaya made clear in his chapter on Japan, teaching factual knowledge is not sufficient. Teachers need to ensure that they are teaching youth these key terms as concepts. This requires active engagement, discussion, and connecting class learning to the world outside of schools.

In all nations, further, there was a strong correlation between having had a significant political experience and more active engagement in political life. Thus, teachers are encouraged to include more inquiry, hands-on learning, or experiential learning in their classes. Teachers can develop experiences that help youth understand their contemporary society and social issues better and connect what they learn in school to their societies and contexts. For example, youth can study a local social or political issue. They can choose an issue that is of interest to them, conduct inquiry to understand the issue better, take trips into the community to learn more about the issue in real life contexts, visit government offices or talk to government officials to see how they address the issue, develop their own solutions to the issue, and try implementing these solutions, in supportive classroom environments (Cargo, Grams, Ottoson, Ward, & Green, 2003).

Educational recommendations also emerge from the Canadian chapter: Young Canadians overwhelmingly supported the election of the young, Liberal Justin Trudeau. Was youth voting based on reactive or reflective thought? Citizenship educators should consider the significance of teaching youth to think critically about their actions. Critical thinking education can teach students skills, such as inquiry, considering diverse opinions, and weighing evidence; dispositions such as open-mindedness; and even a critical orientation to one's own society (Norris & Ennis, 1989; Papastephanou & Angeli, 2007). However, as discussed above, this requires a social and political civic culture that allows for such critical mindedness. It is unclear how this form of education can occur in nations that lack civil or human rights.

Those youth who valued democracy were also more likely to be active. In some cases, those who had more negative attitudes to their own democracies due to the youth's concerns with political scandals were also active. Youth expressed awareness of political corruption and social inequality and greed. Thus, emotional engagement either through like or dislike of government appears to affect engagement, if there is not a fear of retaliation or a sense of futility.

External factors also influenced youth's civic attitudes and behaviors. In particular, family behaviors influenced youth. Youth whose parents were more active civically were usually more active themselves. Youth's political knowledge, acquired in schools or through families, context or social media, further, could influence their actions, sometimes in new ways. For example, youth in Italy are finding new ways of getting involved due to their perception of their limited efficacy through traditional means. Youth may be constructing new forms of civic identity and engagement using new technologies.

In all nations, having had a memorable political experience was related to more active civic engagement. This was apparent in the Hong Kong chapter where contextual changes—the Handover of Hong Kong back to China—were associated with increased youth political activity. Family background, civic knowledge, and memorable political experiences were all found to be significant influences on youth civic engagement across the nations studied in this book.

When asked to describe the characteristics of citizens, in addition, most youth demonstrated acceptance for diverse lifestyles, but felt that citizens should productively contribute to their society through work, respecting the laws and caring about the common wellbeing. In pluralistic nations such as Canada and England, youth did not feel strongly that citizens had to be born in the country or to share the same lifestyles as they did. Youth in some nations that do not identify themselves as being pluralistic sometimes placed more emphasis on citizenship as a birth right. Growing up in pluralist societies that accept diverse immigrants and have a policy of embracing pluralism appears to increase acceptance of diversity.

Italy is currently working through tensions associated with increased pluralism in its society. The Italian study identified that political positions influenced beliefs: those on the right side of the political spectrum were less accepting of pluralism than those on the left.

Overall, we can conclude that the chapters in this book do support a dynamic model of youth civic engagement, and that some internal and external factors influence youth attitudes and behaviors. Further, youth are engaged in their nations or societies in varied ways, depending on contexts and conditions, appearing to make decisions on their type and level of engagement based on these factors.

DISCUSSION: CITIZENSHIP AS A WAY OF THINKING AND BEING

In Chap. 1 , we described citizenship as related to a feeling of belonging to a national or social group. Our Hong Kong-China chapter illustrated how citizenship as a sense of belonging is a function of its social context and how national borders do not necessarily equate to citizenship. The definition given in Chap. 1 is one form of citizenship associated with the rise of nation states. As physical spaces were consolidated into nations in Europe and America, governments felt a need to unite diverse peoples and communities under a common sense of belonging. Thus, we see in Canada a concerted effort to develop and tell nation-building stories through school texts as a way of building this common association (Francis, 1997). In this sense, citizenship education is interwoven with developing patriotism or national association to a particular social group or space. We have citizens connected to an "imagined community" (Anderson, 1991). Wertsch's (2002) work on collective memory, identity, and history in Russia illustrates how attempts to develop national identity can structure how individuals come to think and function and influence how youth are taught in schools.

The development of nation states was tied to the emergence of democracy as a form of government. With roots in the Enlightenment and people's struggle for political representation, nationalism and democracy became intricately woven together: the nation was composed of its citizens and it was these same citizens who governed. Thus, citizenship was participation in democracy. Inherent within democracy is a belief in the potential of "common" men and women to be their own government. Democracy thus requires civic rights, those legal rights protecting citizens such as property rights and freedom of speech, political rights, such as voting rights, and social rights, those rights that protect citizens' welfare (Marshall, 1950). This form of democracy has also been related to capitalism (Marshall, 1950), perhaps as economic wellbeing seems to relate to stronger democracies.

Citizenship associated with nationalism, democracy, and capitalism is a particular discourse, often connected to the nation state or to a particular social group, in places with links to Western legacies. The nation state or society is to be formulated and fostered consciously through the populace's engagement through such actions as participating in their social or political community.

In our globalized world, ideas move through space and time through social media, the internet, and the various outlets of pop culture. An interesting finding of this book is how this democracy-nationalism citizenship discourse is found in a number of nations. Educated youth in places with varied experiences with democracy, including Canada, Italy, India, Mexico, England, Japan, and Hong Kong, illustrate awareness of this discourse and embrace it to an extent. Youth express positive attitudes to democracy, feel that people should be active, view active engagement to encompass voting and volunteering, and are active to limited extents themselves due to such self-identified factors as time or feelings of efficacy. When youth feel that something is important or relevant to them, they can be motivated to become active, as described for youth in Canada and Hong Kong. Attitudes that are supportive of democracy, interest in the news, and participation in discussions through social media are all forms of engagement.

This democracy-nationalism citizenship discourse is made most visible in the chapters on Hong Kong and India. Hong Kong citizens have had a different history and experience with democracy to that of mainland China as they have been colonized by the British. Under British rule, they were introduced to democratic ideas including civic, political, and social rights. Now, they are a special administrative region (SAR) of mainland China, a state known to have one-party rule. In India, we learn about another citizenship discourse as a form of compassion or humanity.

The youth who participated in the research studies described in this book were primarily youth attending university. We can draw some assumptions that many of these youth come from middle class or wealthy families in which they have certain social advantages and possibilities. The similarities youth in varied locations with connections to democracy share in their views about citizenship illustrate this to be a discourse that transcends spatial borders. It may be a discourse of an educated elite, a global class with education and opportunities, connected to and informed through social media (Apple, Kenway, & Singh, 2005; Bauman, 1998).

Further research can explore whether youth with varied backgrounds in these nations/societies also embrace this democracy-nationalism citizenship discourse. As other studies have found that less educated individuals participate less (Howe, 2010), it is possible that youth who do not go on to university may hold different understandings of what good citizenship entails. Social justice theorists comment on the unequal distribution of power in all nations and the manner in which some individuals have greater opportunities than others due to historical and contemporary factors, such as social or cultural capital (Bourdieu & Passeron, 1990). Language, family and cultural background, economic resources, and educational experiences may all influence individuals' opportunities, attitudes, and actions. As this book has argued that context influences thoughts and actions, it is possible that individuals in different social spaces within the same places will hold varied views and actions.

We can consider this democracy-nationalism citizenship discourse to be an ideological force of globalization on its own, and one that is used in justification against terrorists:

> The war we fight today is more than a military conflict; it is the decisive ideological struggle of the 21st century. On one side are those who believe in the values of freedom and moderation—the right of all people to speak, and workshop and live in liberty. And on the other side are those driven by the values of tyranny and extremism. (Bush, 2006, p. 1582)

The democracy-nationalism citizenship discourse identified in many chapters of this book is rooted in particular contexts and histories. Indeed, as discussed, democracy requires a particular civic culture in order to flourish, and does not exist in name only. It is not easy to foster. The following section of this chapter, written by a young adult, aged 22, from Mexico, illustrates how young adults are intelligently aware of their societies and contexts and the challenges that exist in trying to foster democracy in certain contexts.

Mexican Democracy

Tania Naanous in Collaboration with the Mexico Research Center for Peace (CIPMEX)

One of the main obstacles that Mexico faces in establishing democracy is that limited rule of law coexists with immense economic and social problems. Political institutions and multi-party representation do not guarantee the interests of society at large. Mexico has made advances in the last few years with the development of laws, institutions, and electoral procedures that have established a new multi-party system. Yet, institutionalized mechanisms and efforts by the federal government have not been enough to overcome structural elements rooted in the political system.

Mexico is formed mainly by youth: around half of the population will be in an active work phase during the next 20 years. This could represent a demographic advantage, but only if the youth and the government can establish a solid foundation based on freedom of speech, employment opportunities, education, and trust in political institutions (IMJUVE, 2013).

History of Politics in Mexico

In July 2000, the National Action Party (PAN, *Partido Accion Nacional*) won the first free and fair presidential election, ending the hegemonic rule of the Institutional Revolutionary Party (PRI, *Partido Revolucionario Institutional*) that had lasted 71 years. There was hope that with a new party in power and the leadership of Vicente Fox, new and stronger institutions would ensure transparency, restrain corruption, and diminish inequality. However, in 2006, Felipe Calderon's election as president was tarnished by allegations of voter fraud. The Party of Democratic Revolution's (PRD, *Partido de la Revolución Democrática*) presidential candidate, Andrés Manuel López Obrador, refused to acknowledge his defeat, denouncing Calderón's win as too narrow to be valid; he had 0.56 % more votes than López Obrador. Trust and confidence in the electoral system were challenged again (COHA, 2011). In addition, Calderon's "war on drugs" has left numerous accounts of human rights violations and a perception of higher insecurity in the country (Garcia de la Garza, 2015).

Democracy, in theory, has the capacity to enhance public accountability and deter abuse of power. Aiming to increase democracy in Mexico, new public institutions have been dedicated to increasing access to information, supervising public resources, and improving the evaluation of public administration, leading to greater transparency and public awareness of the issues facing Mexico's government. Paradoxically, the more these new democratic institutions advance and are established, the more they heighten the perception that Mexico has failed to win its battle against government corruption, party domination of public offices, and ineffective public administration (Merino, 2012). Factors such as poverty and inequality, corruption, distrust of government, impunity, and increased violence perpetuated by organized crime are factors that still remain unresolved (IFE, 2014).

For many, the election of 2000 only meant the substitution of one corrupt politician for another. This might explain the return of the PRI to the presidency after only two consecutive terms of the PAN (Garcia de la Garza, 2015). In 2012, Enrique Peña Nieto from the PRI was elected president of Mexico. At the beginning, his ambitious economic reform agenda was highly praised by foreign media and international investors. But this did not last long. More than three years into his presidency, his popularity has reached a record low and his international reputation has decreased dramatically. Three main events have tarnished his standing: his luxury home built by a government contractor; drug lord Joaquín "El Chapo" Guzmán's extraordinary prison escape in July 2015, and the "bungled government investigation" of the 2014 disappearance, and likely massacre, of 43 rural students in Guerrero (Estevez, 2015). These events are separate but not independent from the structural problems of the country: 55 million people in Mexico live in poverty (CONEVAL, 2015), the educational system is not equitable, and there are 2.4 million unemployed Mexicans (OIT, 2015). With these numbers, it has been hard for youth to find their place in the political arena. For the majority, reality has fallen short of the president's election promises (Watson, 2016). Further, after the scandal of Peña Nieto´s house, Mexico's Congress approved the creation of an anti-corruption system in 2015. But there are many who feel that reform does not address Mexico's problems of impunity. Statistics show that 99 % of the crimes in Mexico remain unsolved. Despite government efforts to clean up its act, Transparency International still rates Mexico as the most corrupt OECD nation (Watson, 2016).

Role of Civil Society

A democracy exists when policy makers and government work together with society. However, citizens have participated in the molding and creation of public policy in Mexico inconsistently and cyclically. Social engagement increases at key times when specific situations concern citizens directly, but then tends to die down with the passing of controversy or scandal of the moment. One example is a movement born at Universidad Iberoamericana, called "#IAm132" (in Spanish #Yo Soy 132) that arose in protest to Peña Nieto on the principle that democracy cannot be bought. #Yo soy 132 became a brand for fighting against corruption, injustice, undemocratic media, and impunity (Carlsen, 2012). Even though the movement had success and it affected Peña Nieto´s campaign, as soon as he won the election, #Yo soy 132 died down.

A new, promising initiative by citizens, mostly youth, is the "Law 3x3" (*Ley 3 de 3*), which aims to oblige politicians at federal and state levels to declare their assets and personal records such as previous jobs, friendships, and taxes. Under Mexican law, people can present a law if the equivalent of 0.13 % of those on the electoral registry support it. Then Congress is obligated to debate and vote on it (Watson, 2016). This movement is gathering signatures in order to make the Law 3x3 a General Law. Today, a few members from Congress and some state governors have voluntarily complied with the 3x3, and this has given them a higher acceptance rate from voters. The importance of 3x3 for Mexican society is based on the fact that it can help to prevent further abuses of public administration, and it illustrates how civil society can gain ground in Mexico.

Youth Perceptions

A 2012 study of 5000 young Mexicans found that almost 90 % of the interviewees were not interested in politics (IMJUVE, 2012). The reasons for this vary, but the more common responses were because of politicians' dishonesty (37 %), lack of interest (22 %), and lack of political understanding (22 %). Many youth think they should only participate in politics when it is an obligation (26 %) or when an injustice happens (15 %). Six percent think they should never engage in politics.

The Mexico Research Center for Peace (CIPMEX) conducted research with young Mexicans in and near Mexico City. It compared the perceptions of younger and older Mexicans to democracy and found that youth mentioned civil participation as a response to problems less often than older participants (Meschoulam et al., 2015). Most youth also mentioned government corruption (96 %) and distrust of government (89 %) more often than older interviewees, whose corresponding figures were 77 % and 69 %. In general, Mexicans distrust their government. Corruption came out as the main factor. These results are startling considering that in the 2012 election, the total number of citizens registered to vote included nearly 24 million young voters between the ages of 18 and 29, representing at least 31 % of voters nation-wide (Cuna Perez, 2012). The following statements reflect Mexican youth's beliefs:

> I don't know. What if the government is organized crime itself? I think there is a thin line between the easy [illegal way] and the governmental way. (female, 23 years old)

They can't put an order and punishment because the same authorities are colluded and they commit a lot of crimes (male, student, 21)

The primary information source used was the television (IMJUVE, 2012; Meschoulam et al., 2015). However, most youth think that the media is colluded with the government and that they lie to serve the government, or even organized crime (Meschoulam et al., 2015):

> In the last administration we could see in the media a lot of information of killing and deaths, or about operations and arrests. Now, we don´t see it as much. I feel that this government has generated a process of hiding things about organized crime or other and that media fill in that rhetoric. I say this basically comparing between this administration and the last one. (female, 28)
> I am very young, but everything I see in the news I don't buy it. Even if they tell me that something bad happened I don't believe it anymore, my head automatically thinks that is a plot of the government. There is not a grade of trust of what they say, so that's why we keep shut, you can´t trust in the authorities, you don't know who to trust. (student, 19)

The The Mexico Research Center for Peace found that more youth (68 %) use social media as an alternative source of information than older Mexicans (Meschoulam et al., 2015):

> I use the social networks –Facebook and Twitter- as an alternative to have a better type of information, in comparison to the traditional media. (female student, 23)
> Sometimes I read on the social networks about drugs; even in Youtube there are very interesting documentaries concerning drug abuse and drug legalization, and I ask myself why aren't they broadcasted on the national TV which is managed by the government? (working male, 21)

Many participants stated they no longer used mass media because it has become less credible than other sources. Others stated that they still have contact with it but that the media does not necessarily mold their values, perceptions, or conceptions (Meschoulam, 2013).

Most mentioned that their perceptions are formed from their own personal experience or from someone close. Oral conversation is valued more than the media due to the lack of trust to government and mass media (Meschoulam, 2013).

In spite of the levels of apathy described in Meschoulam et al., 2015, half of the interviewees did mention participation as a solution to national problems:

> It is possible to change, but it requires a lot of effort to change the culture of the country from the bottom and this implies a greater involvement of civil society and that is open to change. It is necessary to end with the apathy and create better disposition from everyone in order to generate a difference. (working female, 27)

Conclusions and Recommendations

The hope that came with more democratic institutions and the election of a new political party near the turn of the twenty-first century has given way to disillusionment over continued political, economic, and social issues, despite some promising social movements. Democracy has continued to be elusive due to corruption, nepotism, impunity, and inequality. Citizens, particularly youth, as discussed, have lost faith in the system. These need to be addressed for a genuine democratic transition.

Policy makers need to reform education, create opportunities, and restore trust in government. The country has the right institutions to guarantee transparency and accountability, but they have to work as designed. Teachers in school and universities should encourage and promote youth involvement, using more motivational methods, so youth can be more interested and active in politics. National security and law enforcement strategies should be accompanied by peace building and grassroots programs that aim to improve social, civic, and political conditions in the nation (Meschoulam, 2013).

Citizenship and Citizenship Education in the Twenty-First Century

Many scholars around the world have decried youth civic disengagement. Are youth actually lacking in their civic engagement, or are they, instead, the product of their internal and external influences in interaction? The youth surveyed in this book, and those described above in the section on Mexico, hold many of the same attitudes and behaviors as their parents, whose engagement is also limited, thus demonstrating that they follow general social norms. As youth's actions reflect those of their social contexts, perhaps we should not blame youth for their apathy, and instead recognize that youth are making decisions on their participation based on what they have learned from their contexts, experiences, families, social media, and schooling. Perhaps, we should look more at the actions of adults in communities whose behaviors may be limited or self-involved, or the actions of politicians, who youth in all nations state they don't trust? Youth described issues with politicians ranging from political scandals and corruption to more repressive methods of managing public opinion, and they learn these views from social media, experiences, and conversation. Is there a general need to consider who runs for office and how their positions in power are managed, as well as to work on fostering social and economic contexts that promote engagement, such as communities with economic opportunities and civil cultures that protect and value civil rights, such as freedom of expression? Perhaps we should consider Plato's (1999) comment that people should be forced to rule, in the sense that people who will put the public's welfare above their own should be pushed to be politicians, and not those who self-select themselves to such positions? In the nations studied in this book, democracy is representative democracy, in the sense that politicians are elected to serve the interests of the public that elects them. Tania Naanous suggests above that limited youth civic engagement relates to issues with political representation. How can these political issues be addressed? Tania Naanous suggests that education that raises awareness and engagement, civil culture, and perhaps even social media are means of addressing this problem. It is important to keep in mind that the youth in the nations that participated in this book described their ideal governments as ones in which democratically elected individuals, who represent the diversity of voices and needs of the nation, put the people's needs and wishes first, and govern in the interests of the people and not themselves.

Youth, further, are engaging in their societies through knowledge of the news and social media use. They demonstrate positive attitudes to democracy and participation. They are active when they feel it is worth doing so. They support the democracy-nationalism citizenship discourse described above. All of these are positive forms of civic engagement.

Perhaps, we should engage in more discussions about the connections between citizenship, democracy, and context, and the role that adults, the community overall, and politicians play? Perhaps, we should consider youth's actions to be thoughtful readings of their contexts?

Citizenship educators can also reflect on possibly new ways youth may be engaging civically in their societies and the emergence of new forms of "societies" or "communities" online. Youth learn about—and interact with—local, national, and global events using social media. Social media opens up new ways for youth to engage civically through online communities that cross national borders (Bennett, Freelon, & Wells, 2010). Transnational networks associated with particular issues and pop culture span the globe, connecting individuals by interest and not physical location. How is this engagement mediated? Are youth engaging critically online? Perhaps, we need to pay more attention to social media and its relation to citizenship as a sense of belonging? These forms of engagement open questions about citizenship education that prepares youth to engage effectively in this complex, interconnected, and globalized world, one in which social media, which has its own inherent biases and discourses, should be subject to critique itself (Apple, Kenway, & Singh, 2005).

Youth also demonstrate awareness and insecurity about the times they are growing up in. Educators may need to pay more attention to building skills needed for critical engagement in challenging and inequitable global times, such as critical thinking, analysis, and inquiry skills, as well as employment skills.

Teachers can also work to continue to foster youth's attitudes of openmindedness and respect for pluralism in an increasingly ethnically mixed and complex world, particularly at a time when terrorist attacks have been on the rise in Europe. Educators can consider how to foster a sense of care and compassion in youth, when some individuals with ideologies that are promoted in opposition to that of democracy and open civil societies attempt to terrorize regular citizens going about their lives. Indeed, it is by not becoming fundamentalist in our thinking, but rather by maintaining openness and compassion for others (Broom, 2010), and an appreciation and respect for civil and human rights as forms of citizenship lived through collective action with others, that we have a chance of beginning to neutralize extremism and hatred.

NOTE

1. This book was meant to have a chapter on democracy in an African nation. I attempted to find colleagues in three nations without success. In the first nation, the collaborator withdrew from the study when she could not get university permission for the study, as the study did not come with funding.

In the second nation, the collaborator did not answer emails after agreeing to take part in the study. In the third nation, colleagues agreed to participate. After university ethics approvals, we went through two national and governmental ethics boards, which charged large fees. The government board stated we had to submit a draft of the chapter to their office. By the time these ethics approvals had come through, there was not a lot of time remaining before the book was to go to press. Students across all faculties at a large university in the country were invited to participate in the online survey. However, only a limited number of students participated. The professors asked me if I could send more money to help them promote the study among students. When I submitted the data analysis for the students who had filled out the survey, the professors wrote back stating that they did not feel these data were sufficient to carry out a statistical analysis, despite the rich comments made by the students. the professors felt that reporting these findings could lead to claims that the research was "propaganda".

References

Anderson, B. (1991). *Imagined communities: Reflections on the origin and spread of nationalism* (Rev. ed.). London and New York: Verso.

Apple, M., Kenway, J., & Singh, M. (2005). *Globalizing education policies, pedagogies, & politics.* New York: Peter Lang.

Bauman, Z. (1998). *Globalization the human consequences.* New York: Columbia University Press.

BBC (2016, February 20). Uganda's president Yoweri Museveni wins fifth term. *BBC News.* Retrieved from http://www.bbc.com/news/world-africa-35620934

Bennett, W., Freelon, D., & Wells, C. (2010). Changing citizen identity and the rise of a participatory media culture. In L. Sherrod, J. Torney-Purta, & C. Flanagan (Eds.), *Handbook of research on civic engagement* (pp. 393–423). Hoboken, NJ: John Wiley & Sons.

Bourdieu, P., & Passeron, J. (1990). *Reproduction in education, society and culture.* London: Sage.

Broom, C. (2010). Conceptualizing and teaching citizenship as humanity. *Citizenship, Social and Economics Education, 9*(3), 147–155.

Broom, C. (2016). Exploring youth civic engagement and disengagement in Canada. *Journal of International Social Studies, 6*(1), 4–22.

Bush, G. W. (2006). *Public papers of the Presidents of The United States George W. Bush.* Washington, DC: Government Printing Office.

Cargo, M., Grams, G., Ottoson, J., Ward, P., & Green, L. (2003). Empowerment as fostering positive youth development and citizenship. *American Journal of Health Behaviour, 27,* S66–S79.

Carlsen L. (2012). Mexico elections protest. *Huffington Post.* Retrieved from http://www.huffingtonpost.com/laura-carlsen/mexico-election-protests_b_1741046.html

Consejo Nacional de Evaluacion de Programas Sociales (CONEVAL). (2015). Retrieved from http://www.coneval.gob.mx

Council on Hemispheric Affairs (COHA). (2011). *Democracy in Mexico: The past, present, and future.* Retrieved from http://www.coha.org/democracy-in-mexico-the-past-present-and-future/

Cuna Pérez, E. (2012). Democracy support among young students in Mexico City. Study on youth citizen disenchantment with the institutions of Mexican democracy. *Polis, 8*(2), 107–151.

Estevez D. (2015). Mexico rejects the NY Times criticism of president's stubborn resistance. *Forbes Press.* Retrieved from http://www.forbes.com/sites/doliaestevez/2016/01/05/mexico-rejects-the-ny-times-criticism-of-presidents-stubborn-resistance-to-accountability/#4ad51e6862c4

Francis, D. (1997). *National dreams: Myth, memory and Canadian history.* Vancouver: Arsenal Pulp Press.

Garcia de la Garza A. (2015). Mexico: Active civil society key to ending culture of impunity. *Open Democracy.* Retrieved from https://www.opendemocracy.net/opensecurity/alejandro-garcia-de-la-garza/mexico-active-civil-society-key-to-ending-culture-of-impun

Instituto Federal Electoral (IFE). (2014). *Informe país sobre la calidad de la ciudadanía.* Retrieved from http://www.ine.mx/archivos2/s/DECEYEC/EducacionCivica/Informe_pais_calidad_ciudadania_IFE_FINAL.pdf

Instituto Mexicano de la Juventud (IMJUVE). (2012). *Encuesta nacional de valores en juventud 2012.* Retrieved from http://www.imjuventud.gob.mx/imgs/uploads/ENVAJ_2012.pdf

Instituto Mexicano de la Juventud (IMJUVE). (2013). *Diagnostico sobre la situación de los jóvenes en México.* Retrieved from http://www.imjuventud.gob.mx/imgs/uploads/Diagnostico_Sobre_Jovenes_En_Mexico.pdf

Marshall, T. H. (1950). *Citizenship and social class and other essays.* Cambridge: Cambridge University Press.

Merino. M. (2012). *The second democratic transition in Mexico: Efforts, obstacles and challenges to Mexico in the quest for a comprehensive, coordinated, consistent form of accountability.* Wilson Center, México Institute. Retrieved from file:///Users/tanianaanous/Downloads/democratic_transition_merino.pdf

Meschoulam, M. (2013). Values, perceptions, conceptions and peacebuilding: A qualitative study in a México City neighborhood. *International Journal of Peace Studies, 19*(2), 21–41.

Meschoulam, M., Hacker, A. J., Carbajal, F., De Benito, C., Blumenkron, C., & Raich, T. (2015). Values, perceptions, and peace building: An expanded qualitative study in Mexico. *International Journal of Peace Studies, 20*, 1 . Retrieved from   https://www.gmu.edu/programs/icar/ijps/Vol20_1/Meschoulam_ Hacker_Carbajal_deBenito_Blumenkron_Raich.pdf.

Norris, S. P., & Ennis, R. H. (1989). *Evaluating critical thinking*. Pacific Grove, CA: Critical Thinking Press & Software.

Organización Internacional del Trabajo. (2015). *Perspectivas sociales y del empleo en el mundo*. Retrieved from http://www.ilo.org/wcmsp5/groups/public/ —dgreports/—dcomm/—publ/documents/publication/wcms_443505.pdf

Papastephanou, M., & Charoula, A. (2007). Critical thinking beyond skill. *Educational Philosophy and Theory, 39*(6), 604–621.

Plato. (1999). *Great dialogues of Plato* (W. H. Rouse, Trans.). New York: Signet. (Original work published circa 386 BC).

Watson K. (2016). People vs politicians: Who can tackle Mexico's corruption? *BBC Press*. Retrieved from http://www.bbc.com/news/world-latin-america-35865948

Wertsch, J. (2002). *Voices of collective remembering*. Cambridge: Cambridge University Press.

INDEX